Celestine Sibley

Dear Store

BOOKS BY CELESTINE SIBLEY

Young'ns
Children, My Children
Jincey
Small Blessings
The Magic Realm of Sally Middleton
Day by Day with Celestine Sibley
Especially at Christmas
A Place Called Sweet Apple
Christmas in Georgia
Peachtree Street, U.S.A.
The Malignant Heart
For All Seasons
The Sweet Apple Gardening Book
Turned Funny

Dear Store

AN AFFECTIONATE
PORTRAIT OF RICH'S

by Celestine Sibley

PEACHTREE PUBLISHERS, LTD.

ATLANTA

For all the men and women of Rich's who,
through the years,
have made it a store of legend.

Published by
Peachtree Publishers, Ltd.
494 Armour Circle, NE
Atlanta, GA 30324

Manufactured in the United States of America
10 9 8 7 6 5 4 3 2

Library of Congress Cataloging-in-Publication Data

Sibley, Celestine.
  Dear store: an affectionate portrait of Rich's / by Celestine
Sibley.
    p. cm.
  Reprint. Originally published: Garden City, N.Y. : Doubleday,
1967
  ISBN 1-56145-000-6
  1. Rich's (Retail store) — History. 2. Department stores —
Georgia-Atlanta-History. I. Title.
HF5465.U6R55   1990
381'.45'0009758231-dc20   90-7289
                                                     CIP

All photographs not otherwise cited are courtesy Rich's
Department Store.

A Note From The Publisher

When this volume was first published in honor of the 1967 centennial celebration of Rich's, it became an instant classic. Southerners had long cherished the legendary department store as a model of gentility and as the very paragon of good business. With book in hand, loyal customers could show the unconvinced proof positive that it was really true—Rich's was more than just a store.

There have been many changes through the years; in the world, in the South, and in Rich's. But through this tribute to the "dear" store, we can see the spirit of people working together and helping the less fortunate and find that these are not such old-fashioned ideas after all.

The little dry goods store that opened in 1867 has grown to include 20 stores throughout the Southeast. Rich's helped usher in the twentieth century and is on the threshold of helping us celebrate the twenty-first. Peachtree is proud to make Celestine Sibley's DEAR STORE available again for all those who remember the Rich's of the past and who look forward with hope to the Rich's of the future.

—July 1990

Contents

CONTENTS

"JUST RICH'S . . . THAT'S ALL"

A man in McDonough, Georgia, told the story and he vowed it happened to a woman from some other small town near Atlanta.

It seems that early in her marriage she bought dining room furniture from the well-known Atlanta department store, Rich's. As time passed she felt a vague dissatisfaction with the furniture and one day, sixteen years later, she was back in the store shopping with her daughter, who was about to be married, and she saw exactly what she wanted.

She rubbed a hand along a chair back, according to the story, and said wistfully, "This is really what I should have bought. But that clerk overpersuaded me and all these years I've lived with dining room furniture that I really didn't like!"

The next day, home in Conyers, Jonesboro, or wherever she lived, the lady answered the doorbell to find a Rich's van in the drive—there to deliver the furniture she liked and to pick up, with the store's apologies, that overzealous clerk's mistake.

A true story?

There's no record of it at Rich's. In fact, you'll find Rich's executives who doubt that it happened. But they can't say for sure and four out of every five Georgians would accept it without question, and go you one better with a story *they've* heard about Rich's.

The point is that Rich's is the kind of store such stories are told about.

It is a store of legend.

In a hundred years it has become like Paul Bunyan and John Henry, those other lovable titans of American folklore, the kind of regional institution that the home folks *enjoy* talking about. And if, in talking to visitors from other places, Georgians weave a little fantasy into their stories, who's to blame them? There are few enough commerical enterprises in this world to inspire fond tales.

As there is a measure of truth in all legend, so there was some basis in fact for the tales of remarkable strength and invincible courage Westerners told about Paul Bunyan and Southerners told of John Henry. So there is perhaps foundation for the widely held premise that beneficent nature set Rich's of Atlanta down on a patch of scorched red clay back in the Bad Times of Reconstruction Days for the express purpose of giving aid and comfort, hope and cheer, to a hard beset populace.

It's not exactly true, as Georgians allege, that you can buy *anything* at Rich's. A mountaineer who wrote in several years ago, enclosing a two-dollar money order and asking the store to dispatch him by Tallulah Falls railroad a good wife—"stout, no snuff dipper"—was disappointed.

Neither can you exchange anything without regard to whether you got it at Rich's. A seven-year-old Atlanta boy failed to swap his new baby sister for a space helmet. The toy buyer, however, touched by his faith in Rich's, sent him the space helmet with the store's compliments and a note strongly recommending baby sisters as practically irreplaceable playthings.

Aside from these two exceptions, it's hard to find any family necessity that Rich's won't sell you, very nearly on your own

terms, or take back and exchange at your slightest whim—
even if, as sometimes happens, you bought it from a competitor.

This is, occasionally to the chagrin of a new and ambitious
clerk, not legend but well-documented fact. Some of the old-
timers in the hosiery department still remember with a touch
of bitterness the World War II years when they took back
hundreds of defective nylons of a brand they didn't even
stock. The bakeshop recalls the mother of a bride who came
back to complain that the wedding cake Rich's sent out had
yellow layers, instead of white, and although every last
crumb of it was eaten, she felt subtly wronged. The bakeshop promptly gave her a cake with white layers—one of the
few cases on record, as Tom Mahoney, author of *The Great
Merchants* wrote—of a person eating her cake and having it,
too.

"Is this a store or a philanthropic institution?" hardheaded
observers have been known to ask.

Georgians and a good number of people in Alabama, Tennessee, Florida, South Carolina, and the points north, east,
south, and west, won't be booby-trapped into an either/or
answer with a question like that.

They say with feeling and complete accuracy: "Why, it's
just Rich's, that's all. There's only one Rich's."

What *is* Rich's?

First, it's a big store—a mighty big store, in which more
than thirteen million people spent close to $150,000,000 last
year. It's Rich's Downtown, an eight-story emporium with
a Store for Homes and a six-level parking garage attached
by the umbilical cord of a glass bridge spanning busy Forsyth
Street. And it's five sibling surburban stores—Rich's Lenox,
Rich's Belvedere, Rich's Cobb, Rich's North DeKalb, and
Rich's Greenbriar.

Rich's is also a bundle of staggering statistics: Space totaling three million square feet . . . twenty-eight floors devoted

to selling, using enough carpeting to cover six city blocks . . . fifty-four escalators moving a distance of 650 miles per day . . . the largest private automatic branch telephone exchange in the South . . . seventeen restaurants, cafeterias, and snack bars, serving fourteen thousand meals a day . . . a fleet of trucks and station wagons that travel over two million miles a year to deliver over a million and a half packages, pieces of furniture, and appliances.

But, of course, people don't get patriotic about statistics, and Georgians are patriotic about Rich's in the way they are patriotic about the weather and the dogwood trees, the Cyclorama and *Gone with the Wind*.

A derisive competitor on his way back to New York after an unsuccessful sortie into Atlanta marts of trade, once charged that to people in the South's Bible Belt Rich's is "the true church."

This is obviously rankest libel but Kitty Lofton, who works in Rich's public relations department, was once astonished to hear the store's name come easily and naturally to the lips of a woman bus rider, seeking a simile for her church.

The woman's companion had a grievance against the pastor of her church, which she aired for blocks as the bus progressed toward town. She concluded by saying that she was not only going to quit his flock but the whole Baptist denomination as well.

Attempting to dissuade her, the seatmate said, "I tell you, I feel about my church the way I feel about Rich's. If there's not something for me in one department, there is in another."

Even to a public relations girl, who looks on the store with the fondest of eyes, that allusion was gratifying.

People write poems to Rich's, particularly at Christmastime and on Rich's birthday. For instance, Mrs. Leila Hardeman, of Decatur, felicitated the store on its ninety-ninth birthday thus:

"Dear friends, we've traveled long together
In winter's cold and summer's weather
I've worn your dresses, hats and shoes
And all the things that one would choose
To give them comfort, style, and grace
And look well dressed in any place
So now that I am 87
And not too far away from Heaven
I hope that you, though 99
For countless years may rise and shine."

An Eastman, Georgia mother looking for a special-type beret for her daughter addressed the store's personal shopper, Penelope Penn, this way:

"It's a long way
From Eastman to Atlanta
And I haven't a sleigh
Like Santa
To whisk me to Rich's and home again
So I'm calling on you, Penelope Penn.
Would you please look around your fabulous store
For a tiny beret for my Angela who's four?
Black velveteen would do quite nicely
Her head measures 20 inches precisely
If you can fill my request
Mail it to this address."

The address followed with this postscript:

"I hope all you nice folks in Atlanta
Are treated well by dear old Santa
May your Christmas be merry and your New Year bright
Angela's calling so I'll say 'Goodnight.'"

Penelope Penn dispatched the beret with this note:

"If we can help in the future
Don't hesitate to call
But in the meantime
Merry Christmas and Happy New Year to all."

One elderly Atlanta woman regularly packs a lunch and goes to spend the day at Rich's. She lives on a small pension so she has little money for shopping, but that doesn't seem to bother her or Rich's. On a divan near the entrance of the swank Specialty Shop, where the well-to-do ladies of the South buy their de Givenchy's and Maurice Rentner's, she sits and sews away on her own loving-hands-at-home, every-stitch-handmade wardrobe. At lunchtime, instead of visiting one of the ten restaurants, cafeterias or snack bars, she opens up a paper shopping bag—a *Rich's* shopping bag—and takes out her sandwich and thermos.

Rich's executives and employees, far from suggesting that the old girl move along, bow and smile cordially when they pass her.

"Oh, it's a delightful store!" the old lady says blissfully. "So friendly. I've been coming here fifty years. I only miss if I'm sick or there's a death in the family."

And then with great dignity, she adds: "I give Rich's what business I have, of course. But it isn't the shopping as much as the sociability that I come for."

Part of what Southerners feel toward Rich's is, of course, civic pride in a luminous local success. But most of it is warmer and more personal. In a hundred years Georgians and Rich's have gone through good times and bad together and the big store has proven itself a staunch and dependable neighbor.

On May 21, 1917 a terrible fire swept northeast Atlanta, wiping out seventy-three blocks containing 1553 homes—a five-million-dollar loss. An old lady who presented the store with a handwritten story, "The History of My Life and Rich's" (on her eighty-first birthday and its ninety-eighth), recalled that Rich's was on hand to offer help in fighting the fire, and clothes and household goods for the dispossessed. She and her children had to seek refuge with relatives elsewhere and Rich's, then a much smaller store on Whitehall

Street, opened up so she and others could get trunks and clothing. ("They sent that trunk to the railroad station for us and three months later, after a stay in the country had settled our nerves a bit, Rich's opened their store a bit early again for us. We bought furniture and Rich's delivered it that afternoon—and we slept in our own home that night!")

During the 1920's the price of cotton fell disastrously for a state geared to the cotton economy. Rich's advertised it would buy five thousand bales from Georgia farmers at a price well above the market. Hundreds took advantage of the offer.

In the bleak depression days of the 1930's Walter Rich picked up his newspaper one morning and read that the City of Atlanta was too broke to pay its schoolteachers. He telephoned the mayor and suggested that the teachers be paid in scrip, which Rich's would cash at full value with no obligation that any of it be spent in the store. It was a gesture of faith in Atlanta's future at a time when the city badly needed it.

In 1945 war-weary troops arrived at Fort McPherson one Saturday afternoon before Labor Day, ready to be discharged on Sunday morning. It was a time of rejoicing for the men and their families, except for one little detail. The Army's vault was time-locked for the weekend and they couldn't get their pay until Tuesday. Rich's promptly opened up its safe and advanced the money for the payroll.

The Winecoff Hotel fire, in which 119 persons died in 1946, was a local tragedy which was felt throughout the nation. As soon as they heard of it Rich's employees and executives went out to help the survivors of the fire and the scores of relatives who started pouring in from all parts of the country to identify and claim the bodies of the dead. Dwight Horton, director of employee activities, and Roswell Smith, chief of the store protection department, spent days with bewildered and bereaved visitors, stood by during the heartbreaking procedure in old Grady Memorial Hospital's morgue, and took to them from the store burial clothes for many of the victims. Mrs. Lutie Cheek, who headed the Penelope Penn personal shopping service for many years before her retirement, took members of her staff and offered help and, in some instances, clothes to women victims of the fire who wandered about the scene of the fire in their nightclothes.

There was little the folks at home could do on June 3, 1962 when 130 outstanding Atlanta and Georgia citizens, who had gone to Europe on an Atlanta Art Association sponsored trip, were killed as their charter plane took off for home at Paris's Orly Airport. Rich's, sorrowing with grief-stricken Georgians, pulled its scheduled Monday morning ad and offered instead the simple, comforting words of the 23rd Psalm. And Richard H. Rich, grandson of Rich's founder and now chairman of its board of directors, spearheaded a drive to build a new arts center as a memorial to those who died.

Georgians don't forget these things. Neither do they forget how handsomely Rich's has shared its profits by giving a radio station to the city and county school system, a permanent clubroom, and a paid executive to the garden clubs, hospital wings, and out-patient clinics, the Emory University School of Business Administration, the lab and electronic computer center at Georgia Tech.

Along with the financially impressive contributions Rich's has made to the community, there are small, infinitely personal neighborly acts which endear the old store to its customers.

There's an old woman who lives in a downtown hotel, alone in the world and not well enough to get out much. She has a daily telephone chat with at least one of Rich's telephone operators about the weather and the day's news. If she needs anything, somebody from Rich's runs over to see about her.

The idea that a busy telephone operator doesn't have time to chat with people is completely foreign in the oddly relaxed atmosphere of that big eighth-floor room "over the clock," where a dozen switchboard operators greet the day with a cheery, "Good morning . . . Rich's!" The pat, stereotyped answer and the brisk effort to unload the caller on somebody else are both taboo here.

"If a customer wants to chat, why, my goodness, we chat!" says Chief Operator Tommie Sears. "If she wants to tell us about some problem she has, of course we listen. If we don't, we might put her through to the wrong department."

Neither do Rich's operators counter with a mechanical, "What department is he in?" when you ask for some employee by name. *They* find out.

Tommie herself made that mistake twenty-three years ago when she had just come up from Dublin, Georgia, where she got her training at the town's telephone exchange. Somebody called up and asked to speak to "Miss Annie Mae."

Tommie might have known a Miss Annie Mae in Dublin but she wasn't that well acquainted at Rich's and to her everlasting humiliation she asked the natural question: "Miss Annie Mae WHO?"

Her fellow operators were aghast and so was the customer, who turned out to be movie actress Norma Shearer.

Everybody, but *everybody*, knew the late great Miss Annie Mae Gallagher, Rich's and the South's Number One fashion arbiter! Even Miss Shearer, who was just in town for her husband's Army tour, had known enough to leave the selection of her new fur coat up to Miss Annie Mae.

Tommie hasn't said "Who?" since and scarcely anything surprises her—even when at the height of a big warehouse sale last spring a frantic young woman called up and cried: "Please find Papa! He's due at the church THIS MINUTE to perform a wedding ceremony and I think he's in refrigerators!"

In a matter of seconds Mrs. Sears had determined that Papa, a well-known local cleric, had absentmindedly forgotten a big church wedding and wandered off to take in Rich's sale. She didn't rest until she knew he was out of refrigerators and back at the church and that the hitching was proceeding without a hitch.

Any day's mail turns up fresh examples of the peculiar rapport that exists between Rich's and its customers.

A woman in the pretty little Cobb County town of Smyrna ("The Jonquil City") will write in to thank Rich's because a driver of one of the big green delivery trucks saw a snake in her yard and stopped to tell her about it and to make sure it was not a poisonous one.

A couple on their way from Ohio to Brooksville, Florida, paused at a neighboring lunch counter for a cup of coffee and fell to talking to Mrs. Lillie Weldon of Rich's hosiery department. Mrs. Weldon couldn't bear the idea of visitors being in Atlanta without seeing Rich's, so she promptly invited the Ohioans to go back to the store with her. They did and had such a good time they wrote Mr. Rich a thank-you note and promised to drop by on *all* their trips between Florida and Ohio.

A Denver schoolteacher writes in to say that she had heard so much about Rich's she felt that she knew the store well enough to ask a favor. She and a friend planned to vacation in Atlanta and they wanted a list of sights to see and advice on what kind of clothes to bring. Anne Poland, Rich's public relations director, dispatched folders, maps, a schedule of Gray Line sightseeing tours, and an invitation to the teacher and her friend to be Rich's guests at lunch while they were in town.

Rich's delivery men are famous for offering help to distressed motorists, but sometimes a distressed hostess needs it worse. So pleased was the lady who lived on historic Big Shanty Road, of Civil War fame, with the help she got from one delivery man that she wrote a thank-you note to Mr. Rich. She expected out-of-town guests and ordered a day-bed. The day it was due she had to dash out to the grocery store. When she came back she saw a card on the doorknob, indicating that Rich's delivery truck had been there, and her heart sank. But as she drew closer she saw the driver had penciled her a note:

"Door was open so we put it where we thought you wanted it. If this is not the right place call Rich's and we will move it for you. We thought you might want it for today delivery. Thanks. Rich's."

"I DID need it for 'today delivery'! Bless your heart!" wrote the lady.

R. B. Eason, who started with Rich's in 1918 when its transportation system was a mule and a wagon and stayed forty years to see air freight pouring in from all parts of the world, described it as that phenomenon, a store that's "really run for the customers."

Nowhere is this truer than in the areas of credit and refund and exchange.

With the advent of a wizard named Frank H. Neely, who came to the store in 1924 as its general manager and stayed on to become chairman of its executive committee, Rich's abolished its adjustment bureau.

Let the customer with a complaint decide what would make her happy, Mr. Neely decreed, and that's the way it's been since. Without batting an eye Rich's people have made fantastic adjustments, traveling on the perhaps quixotic theory that the world is made up of mostly honest people, who wouldn't dream of asking anything unfair. Sometimes a clerk taking back a clumsily altered or worn-out garment of OPA vintage might be inclined to question the theory. And sometimes executives of other stores dispute it. But Rich's defends its policy to the death with the most telling of all weapons— sales figures.

Mr. Eason, the veteran transportation man, once did a stint in customer service and he recalls times when he directed adjustments where adjustments didn't seem possible.

When radio was new back in the 1920's, a Rich's customer bought one and then complained that its tempo switch, a familiar fixture on the Victrola, was missing.

"I want it slowed down!" she wailed to Mr. Eason.

He made a stab at explaining the difference between radio and phonographs but the customer wouldn't have it.

"You just send somebody out here and slow this thing down!" she insisted.

Mr. Eason knew he was licked. He instructed the repairman, Tony, to go out and fiddle with the dial until he found a radio station which offered a more sedate style of music and conversation. The repairman was dubious but he did it and the customer was content.

Sometimes an emergency middle-of-the-night exchange is called for and Rich's people grit their teeth and smilingly fall to, as in the case of the young Cartersville father who discovered he had the wrong gauge track for his son's Christmas train. He made this discovery at 2 A.M. on Christmas Day and he didn't hesitate to pull Bennett Tuck, vice president in charge of customer service, from a warm bed to tell him about it.

"I didn't have the nerve to get anybody else up to handle it," confessed Mr. Tuck. "Besides, we needed the train to be sure we had the right track. I told him I'd meet him at the store as soon as he could get there. The night watchman let us into the toy department and we found that the only track left that would fit his train was bolted down in a display. I went down to the hardware department and borrowed a screwdriver, took the track loose, and gave it to him."

Mr. Tuck got back home at 4:30 A.M.—but not to bed. His arrival inadvertently set off his own youngsters.

As for the young father's dilemma being a bona fide emergency, Mr. Tuck didn't question it. Especially when he learned that the little boy involved was a year old and it was his *first* train. Rich's wouldn't want to foul up on a milestone like that.

Credit at Rich's is so easy come by that it's a poor Georgian indeed who doesn't have a Rich's credit card plate. At last count the store had four hundred thousand charge customers and was acquiring new ones every day. Some of them are like the socialite who telephones from England to have her Norman Norell dresses dispatched to her there. The bulk are from the great middle class who buy life's necessaries and pay for them faithfully. But none of these is more beloved to Credit Manager George L. Griffeth than the low-paid domestic workers and laborers, the struggling schoolteachers, the white collar workers who earn little and dream big. It's his and Rich's triumph, too, when a poor Negro schoolteacher finally pays for a grand piano for her musically inclined daughter and the daughter goes forth to make a name for herself on the concert stage.

People are always coming to Atlanta to study Rich's. Several times a year merchandising majors from eastern universities drop by to look at the store and try to learn what makes it the unique but obviously flourishing concern that it is. A dozen mystified Japanese merchants spent several days there last spring, trying to unriddle the curious paradox of a store that will, for instance, spend thousands of dollars to light a Christmas tree and present carolers before two hundred thousand persons, when its doors are closed and there isn't so much as a pocket handkerchief for sale.

The answer was a hundred years a-building.

2

THE FOUNDING

Morris Rich was but twenty years old and Atlanta, by that
name, was the same age when they cast their lots together
in the spring of 1867.

Morris was born in the ancient and strife-ridden city of
Kaschau, Hungary in 1847, the year the bumptious little
frontier town across the sea proudly incorporated itself as a
city of two thousand population and changed its name from
Marthasville (formerly Terminus) to Atlanta.

In addition to their youth, the German Jewish boy and
the little American town had another thing in common.
War had taken a hand in their destiny.

The part of Europe where Morris was born (Kaschau by
its German name, Kassa or Kosice by other names) had been
involved in turmoil, political and military, since it was
founded as a fortress in the fourteenth century. By the time
Morris, born Reich, son of Joseph and Rose Reich, was a year
old, the Revolution of 1848 had started in France, spread
to the rest of Europe, and "Napoleon the Little," nephew
of the great Napoleon I, had his foot in the road, striving
for new territory. Sick unto death of war and its constant
drain on their young manhood and their economy, Europeans
started a wholesale migration to the New World, which was
to catch up young Morris.

Joseph and Rose Reich had seven children, five sons and

two daughters, and an apparently well-thought-out plan for getting them to America. The first to come, in 1859, was the eldest, William, and the fourth son, Morris, twelve years old.

It was in many ways a fearful adventure but a proud one the day Joseph and Rose handed their savings to the two boys and saw them off on the stagecoach to Vienna. In Vienna the two took a train for Berlin and thence to Hamburg, a wearisome, exciting distance of 750 miles. In Hamburg they had to spend some time arranging passage on a ship bound for New York and then they spent three homesick, seasick, cold and hungry weeks in steerage, where their fellow passengers included cattle, goats, pigs, sheep, and a great many equally homesick and seasick human beings.

The brothers, like many Europeans, fortunately had friends and neighbors who had preceded them to this country. The Schwartz family, who later Anglicized their name to Black, as the Reichs were to become Rich, had migrated from Kaschau earlier and were established in Cleveland, Ohio. William and Morris, doubtless confused and bewildered by the melting pot of New York, made for the home of their friends, where they were welcomed, fed, and subsequently launched on their own with jobs in a Cleveland store and a room in a nearby boarding house.

The Rich boys held a variety of jobs. For that time and with little formal schooling available to them, they were apparently well educated. They mastered English so rapidly after they came to this country that nobody remembers ever hearing them speak with a trace of their native German accent. William had served an apprenticeship as a jeweler in Hungary and Morris received some training as a watchmaker, but there must have been little demand for these skills in a country at war. And this New World, like the old one they had left, was rushing headlong toward a bitter four-year war, even as the young Richs arrived. So they did what many another

famous American entrepreneur of that time did—they became peddlers.

The boys had been in this country three years when the
second shift of Reichs from Hungary arrived—Daniel, nineteen, and Emanuel, thirteen. They, too, made for the Mid-
west and began their Americanization and their apprenticeship in the mercantile field.

As soon as the Civil War ended and they were free to
travel South, the four Rich boys struck out. William, the
eldest, the venturesome one, the fortune-maker and -loser, the
family gambler, was the first one to be attracted by Atlanta.
Morris dropped out of the party at Chattanooga, Tennessee,
and got a job in a store. Daniel and young Emanuel headed
for the little town of Albany in south Georgia, where they
opened a store. William made a start with a wholesale drygoods business in Atlanta. He was later to have a whiskey
distillery on Broad Street, an interest in coal mines, and settle
down to rearing eleven children in Nashville, Tennessee.

But in 1865 he had a business and a home in Atlanta,
a stopover spot for young Morris, who soon gave up his job
in the Chattanooga store and returned to peddling with the
entire state of Georgia as his territory. For a year and a half
Morris traveled through the Georgia countryside, taking to
their doors goods the like of which war-starved citizens hadn't
seen since long before Sherman's march to the sea.

When he stopped in Atlanta something about the little
war-scarred, determinedly rebuilding town must have appealed to Morris. For in 1867 he decided to stay.

He borrowed five hundred dollars from William and rented
a rough little building down by the railroad tracks. It had a
number, 36 Whitehall Street, and today it would be cheek by
jowl with the pretty little over-the-tracks area of grass and
flowers, Plaza Park.

In 1867 there was little that was beautiful to look at in
Atlanta.

Little more than two years had passed since the Battle of

Atlanta, when the most utter desolation ever visited on an American city by war had leveled the little town.

In the fall of 1864, after a long hot summer's siege, Atlanta, already a little shell-torn and singed around the edges by departing Confederate forces blowing up their ammunition dumps, had then received the torch-toting forces of General William Tecumseh Sherman. The city was evacuated by order of Sherman in September and after federal occupation of two months, burned and left for dead in November.

Curiously enough, its citizens couldn't wait to get back. Sherman had scarcely turned his back and the fires were still smoldering when people started returning, assessing the damage, sifting through the ashes for their belongings, collecting odd bits and pieces of building materials and beginning to rebuild. Whitehall Street, where Morris was to set up shop, had been a main business street. A reporter for the Atlanta *Daily Intelligencer*, which had refugeed to Macon, returned and cased the situation three weeks after Sherman's departure. He wrote that Whitehall Street was "an entire ruin" except for one block.

"Those acquainted with the city," he went on, "will know what amount of destruction this implies. Full one-half the business houses of Atlanta are included in this count."

Surprisingly, Sherman's men had spared that one block, running from Mitchell to the present Trinity Avenue, because of two old gentlemen who lived there, one of them in a dying condition.

The *Intelligencer* report made a moving and systematic inventory of the damage, street by street, and summed up:

"The stillness of the grave for weeks reigned over this once bustling, noisy city. No whistle from railroad engines, no crowing of cocks, no grunting of hogs, no braying of mules, no lowing of cows, no whirring of machinery, no sound of hammer and saw—nothing but the howling of dogs was heard in our midst.

"The human voice was hushed in our streets, no pedestrians on Whitehall, no children in the streets, no drays, no wagons, no glorious sound of the Gospel in the churches; the theater was hushed in the silence to death. Ruin, universal ruin, was the exclamation of all. . . . We can only liken Atlanta to Moscow after her own citizens had fired it; but a merciful God has not suffered it to be like Babylon and Tyre, like Thebes or Palmyra. The energy for which her citizens have been distinguished has already begun to manifest itself."

All around him that spring of 1867 Morris saw that much-vaunted Atlanta energy at work.

The population had already surpassed that of pre-war Atlanta, reaching a total of 20,288 persons, of whom, sadly enough, 928 were the widows and orphans of Confederate soldiers. The city limits had been extended to enclose a circle three miles in diameter. The city treasury, down to $1.64 at the end of the war, was burgeoning with $29,000, and the city directory estimated the number of stores on business streets at 250—"mostly brick buildings."

Morris's little store was not brick but a crude twenty-by-seventy-five-foot structure thrown together from rough-hewn pine boards. There were plenty others like it, hastily built stores and houses and "calico" fences woven from odds and ends to keep wandering livestock out of gardens that were now needed more than ever.

Once when he was an old man Morris recalled for an interviewer that the day he opened his store it had been raining and Whitehall Street was a mire. He went out and laid boards over the red clay mud to protect the footwear of the customers he hoped would come.

That was May 28, 1867.

And the customers did come. Young Morris and a cousin, Adolph Teitlebaum, who had come to work for him, put in long hours in the store. Their strong sellers were fifty-cent corsets and twenty-five-cent stockings, for the women of Atlanta had little money for finery in those days. Even those who had been accustomed to nice things were now lucky to get the practical necessities. Homes were burned, servants freed, horses and carriages were no more, and old letters of the day reflect that many of the erstwhile stylish were engrossed in that day with such mundane, pioneer-type problems as what happened to the old iron washpot.

Morris accommodated himself to the times, selling for money when he could get it and cheerfully taking chickens and eggs and corn in exchange for drygoods when barter was necessary.

Many a night the gas street lights, newly restored to the city, would be burning when Morris left the store and walked toward William's house, gingerly bearing a basket of eggs or a mess of turnip sallet from the day's receipts.

What the slender dark-eyed youth saw in this frenetic young American city was far different from the European home of his childhood. Even in 1859, when he left it, Kaschau had been bigger. It had a population of fifty thousand people then and many beautiful, centuries-old buildings. But Atlanta had what he had, youth and vitality, and that was undeniably appealing.

When the first citizens came back to town after Sherman's departure the gaunt silhouettes of blackened chimneys, and roofless, floorless stone walls epitomized the general desolation. Wryly the townspeople with humor that survived even adversity called them "Sherman's Sentinels" and "Sherman's Monuments." And then being practical people, possessed of that famous energy, they went to work to see how much of the secondhand brick and fire-seasoned rock could be reused. They were still pulling down chimneys and walls when Morris launched his enterprise. Drays loaded with lumber rattled by all day and until far into the night. From hand-pushed barrows Confederate veterans, who no longer had horses or wagons, hawked firewood which they had cut in the forests. (Historians say that what war failed to do to destroy the beautiful virgin forests around Atlanta the firewood vendors finished.)

There were several drygoods stores bigger and finer than Morris's little beginning. W. A. Moore and E. W. Marsh, merchants who had operated in Atlanta before the war, were back and operating again. C. E. Boynton, a successful merchant, and his partner, E. P. Chamberlin, were back and beginning to rebuild. (They were later to be Morris's chief competitors for the carriage trade.) M. C. and J. F. Kiser were on their way from Campbell County to establish what the old historian, E. Y. Clarke, described as "the immense wholesale dry goods house." (William's was apparently too small to warrant Clarke's attention at the time.)

There were several banks, among them the Atlanta National, founded in General Alfred Austell's home in September 1865 and the forerunner of the present First National. Up Whitehall Street between Hunter and Mitchell streets "at the sign of the Mill Saw and Game Cock," as it advertised, there was a small hardware store which a couple of years later would change its name from Tommey & Stewart to a name well known a century later—Beck & Gregg Hardware Company.

Another neighbor on Whitehall Street was the shop of German-born Charles Heinz and his brother-in-law, John Berkele, offering "at the sign of the Big Gun" such commodities as "guns, rifles, pistols, carpenters' tools, and light hardware." Berkele would later help launch the jewelry firm, Maier and Berkele.

Hotels were going up, and many of the mansard-roofed, jigsaw-ornamented houses of the Victorian era were emerging from rubble and mud. Fire protection was restored and the city made a fete out of naming the new steamer fire bell. They decked the steamer with garlands of roses, put her on public display—"the cynosure of all eyes"—and had her christened at the peak of a "Full Dress Hop" by a local belle, Miss Emma Latimer. The fire alarm bell, which was later to toll the death of such notables as Ben Hill, the Civil War general-statesman, Alexander Stephens, Confederate

Vice President, and the *Constitution* editor, Henry W. Grady, was hoisted to its tower "amid loud huzzahs and an enlivening strain of music from Professor Clark's Silver band." Miss Augusta Hill dedicated it.

Along about the same time the *Daily Intelligencer* noted another innovation in fire fighting. Horses, instead of men, had been obtained to pull the fire steamer for Mechanic Fire Company No. 2—"a splendid pair of gray horses, over sixteen hands high, to be attached to their little steamer on the occasion of conflagrations."

In spite of the little city's preoccupation with building, there was trouble. Crime was a problem. Bands of rowdies roamed the streets. Robbery and murder happened frequently. And the political situation infuriated the townspeople.

Morris, who was not to become a naturalized citizen for several years, was no worse off than hundreds of native sons who were deprived of their rights by their participation in the late war. Everywhere he saw signs of lawyers offering to seek pardons for the disfranchised.

Military rule had been suspended for a time, but the Congress of 1867 passed a new Reconstruction Act over President Johnson's veto—a measure ordained by radicals and filling Southerners with consternation.

In May 1867, even as Morris opened his store, military rule was restored to Atlanta. Major General John Pope, a West Pointer from Illinois, was military governor of Georgia, Alabama, and Florida. He was ensconced in the National Hotel, given a banquet and a concert . . . and watched.

Atlantans hoped that Pope was a sensible man and were willing to give him the benefit of the doubt, but he was destined to lose the respect of the majority of Georgians before he was relieved of his command in December of 1867. He was succeeded by Major General George Gordon Meade, who also started out auspiciously by toasting the Confederate General John B. Gordon, his former enemy.

A reporter covering his arrival gave the new military governor what amounted to an extravagant, southern-style compliment. He was, wrote a reporter for the Atlanta *New Era*, "pleasing in appearance and attractive socially—more like a Virginia gentleman than a soldier." His popularity unfortunately was also short-lived.

A great deal of this was of slight interest to the young immigrant boy, trying manfully to keep his store going, but some of the things he saw and remembered all his life. Among the hordes of new people who poured into Atlanta from the North and the West there were two kinds—contributing citizens who gave to the city, and the despised carpetbaggers who came solely for their personal gain and were ruthless about exploiting a helpless and hard-pressed people.

Morris, although young, set the course which his family and his enterprise were to follow for a hundred years. He chose to be a part of Atlanta and to share what he had—and he expressed it in his merchant's way by extending credit to those who needed it, probably worse in 1867 than they ever would again. It wasn't easy because he had little capital to work with, but he accepted the time-honored custom of letting country people settle up their bills once a year—"when the cotton comes in"—and he went on from there.

3

THE FAMILY

Atlantans may not know more about the route to the hereafter than most people but they are fond of repeating what a seasoned and probably weary air traveler once said.

"When you die," he observed, "it matters not whether you're headed for heaven or hell, you'll have to change planes at the Atlanta airport."

In 1877 some coal-smoked fellow with a cinder in his eye probably expressed the same sentiment but said instead, "You'll have to change trains in Atlanta."

When Morris Rich had been in Atlanta ten years the railroads had recovered from the ministrations of Sherman's men, who had ripped up crossties and burned them to heat the rails, which were then bent and twisted, they hoped, beyond use.

But, of course, rebuilding Georgians did use them, until rolling mills were established and they could get new rails. They heated them and straightened them as best they could, with the result that for several years after the war there were "scrub-board" stretches of road, where riding was so rough passengers wished they could get off and walk, and derailments were frequent.

By 1877 old roads had been mended and new ones were advancing in all directions. The Western and Atlantic went west and north; the Georgia railroad provided connections east and north; the Macon and Western reached the southern seaboard, opening up the southwest; the Richmond Air Line went into northeast Georgia and the Carolinas, and the Georgia Western was almost completed to the coal fields of Alabama.

Atlanta was booming as a marketing and distribution center, a natural crossroads between the grain- and stock-raising regions of the north and the cotton-, tobacco-, and rice-raising regions to the south.

Quick to make the most of this situation, it took itself a pseudonym, "The Gate City of the South," and launched a successful campaign to take the state capital away from the old town of Milledgeville down in middle Georgia. (Voters of the state ratified the move in a constitutional amendment in 1868.)

Morris Rich, now a mature thirty years old, had prospered. He had already expanded sufficiently to move twice—to 43 Whitehall Street and then to 65 Whitehall at the corner of Hunter. Each move brought a bigger store and a bigger stock and was heralded by a lively volley of advertising, which Morris liked from the first and which Rich's, the store, would, with the passing years, perfect as an art.

Personally, Morris must have been much happier because he had a strong and warm attachment for family and his was rapidly surrounding him.

Everybody but his father, Joseph, had come over from Hungary by that time. A brother, Herman, had settled in Birmingham. His older sister, Julia, married in Hungary, had arrived with her husband, J. Hirshberg, and their youngest sister, Fanny. And the mother, Rose, had preceded her husband to this country, dying in 1875 at the age of fifty-eight years—five years before Joseph would arrive in 1880. (She is buried in Oakland Cemetery and Joseph, who died in 1885 at the age of seventy-five, is buried nearby.)

Best of all, Morris's South Georgia brothers, Emanuel and Daniel, had disposed of their store in Albany, brought their stock to Atlanta to pool it with his, and were coming into the store with him. Both started as clerks and in February 1877 Morris took an ad in the *Constitution* to announce a new partnership.

The little store was no longer "M. Rich" but "M. Rich & Bro."

(Daniel advanced to status of partner July 1, 1884, when the store became M. Rich & Bros.)

Life was no longer all work for the Rich brothers. There was time for social activity, and the Jewish community to which they belonged in Atlanta sprang from a rich European culture in many ways more sophisticated and more advanced than that of the rest of the area. There were intellectuals in the group, people of cultivated tastes and breeding and a lively interest in entertaining.

A congregation had been organized back in 1867, when a visiting rabbi, here to officiate at the wedding of Abram Rosenfeld and Miss Emilie Baer, urged the guests to form a congregation and to engage a rabbi. William Rich was a charter member of the group, which met first in homes and then in rented rooms over store buildings until 1877, when its first synagogue was completed at the corner of Forsyth and Garnett streets.

Except for William, the Rich brothers in Atlanta were bachelors. (William was married to Miss Rose Loveman of Nashville, Tennessee, and subsequently went there to live.) They were well established in business and eminently eligible.

Such a situation has ever presented a challenge to the women in a family and to friends with matchmaking propensities. The Rich brothers' friends and relations were no exception.

They caught the three bachelors up in a surge of party-giving and party-going, in introductions and social encounters that could but lead to matrimony for all three of them in the space of a couple of years.

These marriages, it happened, supplied new branches to a

family tree of such spread it has reached almost every phase of Atlanta business, professional, and civic life. The descendants of the Richs and their connections by marriage today include scores of prominent Atlantans who have made significant contributions to the life of the community.

It happened that Morris was the first of the trio to succumb to romance.

Miss Maud Goldberg, the attractive daughter of Rachel Solomon Goldberg and Marcus Goldberg, of Madison, Georgia, stopped off to visit friends in Atlanta on her way home from school in St. Louis in 1877. The matchmakers saw that she and Morris met and in less than a year, on February 28, 1878, they were married.

It was a marriage which was to endure for fifty years—until Morris's death in 1928. As a Rich's employee wrote in the store paper, *Rich Bits*, in 1925: "A happy homelife is another of his successes in life. When we see Mr. and Mrs. Morris Rich together our organization feels a thrill of pride that they belong to us."

Emanuel and Daniel were to follow suit within a year.

Morris Adler, founder of the Atlanta Paper Company and a native of Germany, had brought a wife from his homeland, the former Elise Sartorius of Frankfurt, Germany. It happened that Mrs. Adler's sisters, Bertha and Claire, came to Georgia to visit her. Bertha captivated Emanuel and in 1879 they were married. (The third Sartorius sister, Claire, was to help found another prominent Georgia family. She was married to Joseph Jacobs, who launched the Jacobs Pharmacy chain, and they became the parents of another distinguished Atlantan, Sinclair Jacobs.)

The same year, 1879, Daniel Rich, eldest of the three, married their first cousin, Julia Teitlebaum, sister of Adolph, who worked for Morris when the store was new.

Subsequently, Fanny, the youngest of the children, would marry Aaron Haas, who had run the Yankee blockade outside Savannah to get Georgia cotton to the British in the Bahamas.

Their children and grandchildren are prominent today in real estate and legal circles in Atlanta.

The young Morris Richs, like many other young marrieds of the time, boarded for a while before establishing their own home, part of the time with Emanuel and Bertha at 57 West Garnett Street. It was here that both couples had their first children in 1880. To the Emanuel Richs was born a little boy, Walter, who would succeed his uncle at the helm of the store in 1926. Morris and Maud's baby was a girl, Rosalind, whose son, Richard Rosenheim (later to be changed to Rich), would take his turn at heading Rich's in 1949.

Before the next babies arrived the Rich brothers had established a unique complex of homes. Emanuel, "the artistic one," designed, and they built three big two-story frame houses next door to one another on Pryor Street near Richardson.

The houses varied only slightly in architectural detail. One of the Morris Richs' granddaughters, Mrs. Louis Montag, heard many times as a girl the story of how the brothers drew straws to see who would get which house.

"All the brothers were close but Emanuel and Morris were nearer the same age and their wives were congenial so they hoped to live next door to each other," she said. "But Daniel drew the middle house."

When the telephone came in Daniel and Julia paid for being in the middle. The brothers decided one telephone was enough for all and they put it in Daniel's house.

Presently the Rich complex housed ten children, two each for Morris and Emanuel and six for Daniel, and it was a merry, sometimes quarrelsome tribe often swelled on weekends by cousins. On rainy days the Richs' delivery wagon came to take the children to school, and Mrs. Morris Rich was later to confess to her grandchildren that she always tried to get her two little girls, Rosalind and Valerie, ready first and out the door so they could sit in the cab with the driver out of the weather.

Julian Hirshberg, grandson of the elder Rich sister, Julia, and a well-known Atlanta investment counselor, remembers vividly the custom of regular weekend calls at Pryor Street.

"We went every Saturday or Sunday," he said. "And our parents were meticulous about alternating the order in which we called. We stopped at the Morris Richs' first one week, the Daniel Richs' first the next, and the Emanuel Richs' first the next."

For years the three Rich brothers walked home together for midday dinner and a nap or rode *The Dummy,* a steam engine-drawn streetcar, which ran down Pryor Street. For years they kept their money in a joint bank account. But marriage may have changed that or perhaps it was William himself, the flamboyant one, who had a taste for investing money in glamorous enterprises such as coal mining. William, according to family lore, was a millionaire four times and broke four times.

Each time the brothers rallied to help him out, and when they hit rough sledding financially or fell out on some issue, it was William who rushed to the scene with money or to act as a peacemaker. William's grandson, Adolph Breyer, now a merchandise manager in Rich's Store for Homes, was reared in Nashville, where most of William's eleven offspring settled. He recalls that it was the most natural thing in the world for the family to assume that when the various cousins went off to school they would stay with the relative closest to that school. One of the Daniel Rich daughters lived in the Breyer household when she attended school in Nashville, and when young Adolph enrolled at Georgia Tech, he checked in at the Daniel Richs'.

Morris's younger daughter, Valerie (Mrs. Percy) Myers, who was to be born in the Pryor Street house in 1884, remembers that her father took pleasure in his home and particularly in his garden. He liked to get up early in the morning and take a horseback ride, returning to get in some time with his fruit trees or working among his vegetables before going to the store. Many Atlantans now old remember a particularly fine fig tree that Morris grew in his backyard, along with raspberries, strawberries, and peaches.

The furnishings of the houses were substantial and comfortable. Emanuel, who became the firm's expert, particularly on Oriental rugs, kept an eye out for special things for all the homes.

But Morris, according to his daughter, had a horror of anything ostentatious. On buying trips to New York he always brought back presents for his wife and something for the house, but it was usually a gift notable for its simplicity.

"He liked to bring my mother jewelry," recalled Mrs. Myers, "but it was always a modest piece of jewelry. It was a time when all of us went in for bric-a-brac and he would bring us something for our collection but it would be on the plain side."

Some native sense of restraint and taste apparently saved Morris from the excesses of an age of opulent geegaws. His wife, Maud, was like-minded.

"My mother was a beautiful woman but very modest," said Mrs. Myers. "When the big hats came into style the milliner at the store tried to put them on her but she would blush and shake her head. She didn't like anything showy."

With such a big family there would seem to be little reason to go beyond it for social activity, and the Morris Richs seldom did. They were among the early members of the Standard Club and Morris sometimes spent an evening playing cards with his men friends. But he liked best of all to spend summer evenings working in his garden and winter evenings reading or playing the violin in his own home.

He had taken up English at night school when he first arrived in Cleveland and thereafter read and spoke English exclusively. Mrs. Myers remembers but one time when the language of his childhood came back to him, and that was on the occasion of her parents' twenty-fifth wedding anniversary when she accompanied them on a trip to Europe. Fragments of Hungarian popped into his head and he proudly used it when he took them to Budapest, which was as close as they came to his old hometown Kaschau, in 1903.

His interest in the violin was that of a talented amateur. He had never had a lesson but he had a good ear, and many an evening lively fiddle tunes floated out of the house on Pryor Street.

While the brothers were establishing homes and families, things were flourishing down on Whitehall Street. In the Sunday *Constitution* of July 2, 1882, they offered for rent "one of the best stores in the city"—the one they occupied at 65 Whitehall.

"They only move," said the advertisement, "because they want more room, which they will get in their new store, 54 and 56 Whitehall Street."

The new store opened the following September, after a series of removal sales at the old building. The *Constitution* saluted the new store as "a bazaar of fashion . . . emporium of fashion and design."

That story in the fulsome prose of the time shows how Atlantans had in a brief fifteen years progressed from the grim exigencies of the postwar days and how Morris and his brothers had earned the affection and respect of the town.

"For years," wrote the *Constitution*, "no house in Atlanta has been better known than that of M. Rich & Bro. The fact that no matter what hour you might be passing, their establishment was always filled with the leading ladies of the city, who know that Rich's could always meet their desires, is the best proof of their stock. In silks and satins, in ladies wear of every character and design, suitable for the raiment of the maid in the kitchen to the gorgeous robes of the bride as she stands before the altar, there is not an article which cannot be supplied by this house. Such profusion of ribbons, such sparkling rows of buttons, such variety and style in the dress goods line it would be impossible to more than duplicate, and there are very few who can do that."

The story continued to describe the building as "a striking picture in its art and architecture," with an interior of "such beauty and design that one is dazzled by the display" . . . a layout "acknowledged by all who have seen it to be the most complete establishment of its kind in the South, New Orleans, even, not to be excepted."

Of the Rich brothers themselves, the newspaper said they "rank high as business men, a reputation which they have won by fair dealing, attention to business and discretion in reading the wants of their customers."

The story ended with an editorial accolade:

"It affords The Constitution pleasure to note the progress of such sterling business men as the Richs. It is due to such men that Atlanta is what she is, and if those in other lines of business hold their own as well as the Richs hold theirs, our progress will still be onward."

4

GROWING CITY, GROWING STATE

For cities in its population class—over 30,000—Atlanta was the fastest-growing in the nation in 1890. In one decade its population had jumped from 37,409 to 65,533, and during the first six months of 1890 houses were built to accommodate 10,000 persons.

It was a merchant's paradise. All those houses had to be furnished, all those people clothed!

M. Rich & Bros. tackled the job as if it were theirs alone, although their competition up and down Whitehall Street was plentiful and stiff. In fact, from the standpoint of floor space and annual sales, Rich's ranked third in 1890. (Chamberlin, Johnson & DuBose Company was the leader and J. M. High ran second.)

But Morris and his brothers were working hard and branching out into many areas. The new Georgia capitol was completed in 1889 and Rich's won the contract for carpeting it—a $10,000 job and a real coup for the store because many larger out-of-state firms had bid on it.

This was the first major job of a whole new department, which today functions in a separate building on Marietta Street. Institutions, which were poor, unlovely places in those days, now are a principal customer, as are motels, which, of course, were unheard of when Georgia's capitol was new.

The fabled Oglethorpe Hotel in Brunswick, designed by

Stanford White and still standing until the 1950's, was also carpeted by Rich's, drawing a letter of commendation from the board of directors. The letter mentioned the capitol job as having also gone to "the wide-awake firm of M. Rich & Bros. . . . who, ever alive to their own interests, and jealous of the good name of Atlanta, put forth their best efforts and succeeded in obtaining the contract for the carpets and draperies for the honor of our progressive city."

Later Rich's was to carpet and furnish the Aragon Hotel, first of the "upper Peachtree" hostelries, situated at the corner of Peachtree and Ellis streets. And still later it was to win the contract for furnishing the late, lamented Piedmont Hotel, which opened in 1903 and held out until 1966.

Of the Piedmont, Rich's said in an ad: "We secured the Furniture Contract for this magnificent hotel against the strongest competition, not only in Atlanta but against the largest stores in New York and Chicago."

They made special note of the brass and iron bedsteads, leather furniture for the lobby, "and handsome mirrors for 140 bathrooms."

But that was in 1903, and as Franklin Garrett in his *Atlanta and Its Environs* noted, in 1890 Atlanta completed a new sewer system but was "still, by more than three to one, a privy town." The new sewer system, hailed by the Board of Health as "The most important sanitary advance ever attempted in the city," did not supplant the twelve, two-horse night-soil wagons which industriously moved through the city cleaning out the backyard facilities of more than five thousand homes.

Even if plumbing facilities of the nineties were largely primitive, the town was growing up.

Georgia Tech held its first commencement in June 1890. Grady Memorial Hospital was dedicated on May 15, 1892 and named for Henry W. Grady, the famed *Constitution* editor and orator, who had died two days before Christmas in 1889. They broke ground for a newly organized college for females in Decatur and named it Agnes Scott in memory of the mother of the most substantial contributor. Electric street cars were put into service. Atlantans played such an enthusiastic part in the return of Democrat Grover Cleveland to office, after the Republican victory in 1888, that one of their number, Hoke Smith, was named Secretary of the Interior, the first Atlantan to hold a cabinet post.

Both President Cleveland and his running mate, Vice President Adlai E. Stevenson, came to town to visit. The Rich's-decorated Aragon Hotel had just opened when the Vice President made his visit and it was the scene of a dance given by H. H. Cabaniss in honor of Mr. Stevenson. Historian Garrett records that real estate along Peachtree Street was skyrocketing even then.

It seems, according to Mr. Garrett, that George Washington Collier, the old settler who ran one of the first stores and the first post office in Atlanta and whose farm subsequently became Sherwood Forest, owned the elegant, six-story Aragon Hotel. An eastern capitalist besought him to sell it but Wash, as his friends called him, wouldn't even put a price on the land.

Finally the would-be buyer asked if he covered the land with silver dollars if that would be sufficient to buy the land. Yes, said Wash, if he stood the dollars on edge. It was no deal, reports Mr. Garrett.

Proof of Atlanta's growing sophistication in the 1890's may be found in a menu from the Aragon: "Cocktails, Manhattan or Martini. Hors d'Oeuvre. Fish course with Sauterne. Roasts with claret. Squabs or chicken with champagne. Demitasse with liqueurs—pousse cafe or creme de menthe."

As sophisticated as it was, Atlanta was sensitive to anything that might be construed as what the lewd literature censors of the future would call "of prurient interest." And Morris Rich was one of a number of prominent Atlantans who were called into Judge Andy Calhoun's police court in November 1894 to judge whether or not a placard advertising the approach of "Airy Fairy Lillian Lewis" to play a role later made famous by Elizabeth Taylor—Cleopatra—was lewd and obscene.

Martin J. Dooley, known as "Dooley the Bill Paster," had plastered the town with eight-foot lithos of the Egyptian queen, who was said to wear gold-buckled garters and to keep a tame lion as a pet.

There are no copies of that placard among the Atlanta Historical Society's art works but Miss Lewis, the "airy fairy" one, addressed a postcard to the *Constitution* saying it was the reproduction of a famous painting by J. Leon Gerome, a celebrated French artist. As such, said the actress, it was not obscene but "high art." Defense Attorney Walter Brown called a roster of men who were ostensibly the town's more cultivated citizens, to pass judgment on the poster in court. The group included, in addition to Morris, the famous author of the Uncle Remus stories, Joel Chandler Harris, *Constitution* publisher Clark Howell, and H. M. Patterson, among others.

There's no record of what Morris thought of the sex queen because the shy, blushing Joel Chandler Harris, who abhorred public appearances of any kind, broke up the court by declaring that he thought the bills were "horrible things," which he wouldn't like to have in his backyard. Asked by the judge what effect "a woman in tights—in blue tights—has on you, Mr. Harris?" the author-editor blushingly stammered, "No effect, sir."

For the record, Judge Calhoun ruled in favor of the poster, holding, says historian Garrett, "that the effect of a fine form could be viewed and enjoyed just as the beauty of a spirited race horse or the neck of a graceful swan."

It was probably Atlanta's first censorship case and one of the few courtroom appearances of Morris Rich.

Certainly the most memorable trip to court for him must have come December 8, 1903 when he went into Superior Court and filed his petition to become a naturalized citizen of the United States. In his petition he "renounced forever all allegiance and fidelity to every foreign Prince, Potentate, State or Sovereignty . . . more particularly the allegiance and fidelity which he in anywise owes to the Emperor of Austria, of whom he was hitherto a subject." He received his final papers in February of 1910.

But before that personally satisfying day should come to him Morris and his brothers proved themselves civic-minded citizens by helping to bail out the debt-ridden Cotton States & International Exposition, which ran for three months in 1895 in what is now Piedmont Park (then the "exposition grounds").

Although financially in the hole like most fairs and expositions, the exposition must have been a recreation and public relations success. President Cleveland officially opened it at sundown September 18, 1895 by pressing a button at his summer home in Buzzards Bay, and a month later he came to Atlanta to visit it. It drew the headline entertainers of the day—Buffalo Bill and his Wild West Show, John Philip Sousa and his band, Walter Damrosch and his Damrosch Opera Company, and Victor Herbert and his orchestra. The famed Negro leader, Booker T. Washington, visited the exposition and spoke in Atlanta. St. Clair McKelway, editor of the Brooklyn *Eagle*, was a speaker. But it ran one hundred thousand dollars in the hole, a sum which Atlanta business leaders, the Richs among them, made up.

All kinds of interesting people were coming to Atlanta in those days—Susan B. Anthony to preside over the twenty-seventh annual gathering of the National American Woman's Suffrage Association; Eugene V. Debs to address a labor meeting; William Jennings Bryan, the defeated candidate for President, and even William McKinley, his successful opponent for the Presidency.

The DeGive opera house was opened in 1893 and called the Grand—now Lowe's Grand—and Anna Held, after bathing in milk in her suite at the Aragon, appeared at the opera house in a disappointingly decorous comedy. James Whitcomb Riley, the Hoosier poet, came to town and is said to have come closer to wowing the Grand audience with his homely verses than Miss Held did with her internationally famous beauty and glamor.

The Confederate Veterans Reunion brought sixty-five thousand persons to Atlanta on July 20, 1898—the biggest crowd of visitors the city had ever accommodated. They came by wagon, on foot, and by train, filling the stores up and down Whitehall Street, the hotels, restaurants, and barrooms. Thousands were fed in a tent-covered commissary at Piedmont Park, and the street-car company reported that it collected eighty thousand nickels in one day. There was a big parade in a downpour of rain, reviewed by General John B. Gordon, and balls, banquets, and speeches. General James Longstreet came for the occasion, as did Mrs. "Stonewall" Jackson and Miss Winnie Davis, "The Daughter of the Confederacy."

Except for a depression in 1893, business was good. The Rich brothers persisted in looking on the bright side, announcing fresh stock, cut prices, and a "standard of excellency that places us as the 'First House in the South' . . . The largest stock! The finest goods! The best values, the lowest prices."

"We are going to have a great fall business," Morris affirmed in an ad, "and calamity howlers can't prevent it. Brace up and take part in the returning tide of prosperity when it comes along. Confidence is now returning and money will be plentiful again within a brief time and banks, merchants, and everybody except the croakers, will be happy."

Emanuel, Morris's younger brother, died in 1897 at the age of forty-eight years. He had been a valued partner in the store for twenty years and before that served as salesman.

His going from the Rich complex on Pryor Street was a profound personal loss to all the family, and his departure from the store left a gap which Morris did not find easy to fill. A young furniture salesman, J. J. Haverty, was placed in charge of Emanuel's favorite carpet department. (Mr. Haverty was later to found a well-known furniture chain of his own.)

But then there was the administrative vacancy which was going to be hard to fill.

After the funeral, Morris, returning to the store, must have looked searchingly at his employees, seeking the ones who showed the talents he was going to need. Two of them impressed him, David H. Strauss, the accountant, and Lucian York, who had started as a clerk in the middle 1880's, demonstrating almost immediately administrative abilities.

Three years later in 1900 M. Rich and Bros. filed a petition for a charter of incorporation. The charter was granted and at the first meeting of the stockholders Morris was elected president, Daniel vice president and treasurer, and David H. Strauss was made secretary. Strauss and William Rich were also members of the board of directors. Mrs. Bertha Rich, widow of Emanuel and mother of Walter, then but a teen-age boy, was one of the incorporators.

It was the beginning of a trend which was to become standard procedure with Rich's. The store, after a hundred years, continues to be one of the few remaining family-run enterprises of size in the country. But since the death of Emanuel, followed by its incorporation, it has enlisted the talents of outstanding outsiders where they could be found.

One of the most dramatically effective teams—David Strauss, Walter Rich, and Frank H. Neely—would come later.

In 1904 Atlanta was reaching the one-hundred-thousand population class and Rich's was growing with it. There were now two Rich's stores on Whitehall Street, connected by corridors, and in the new, pushing city Rich's properly regarded itself as an old settler. In celebration of its "thirty-seven years of progress" it quoted in an ad the late *Constitution* humorist, Bill Arp, as saying, "Wherever I go from Texas to Florida, I hear the name Rich's spoken in every household in terms of praise and appreciation."

Rich's was branching out in a mail order business, and by 1906 announcing plans for a new store at 52-54-56 Whitehall—a store which would be finished and ready for occupancy on Saturday, January 12, 1907.

So impressive was this new store that the Atlanta *Journal* pulled out all the stops on a news story headlined, "The Magnificent New Department Store of M. Rich & Bros. Co., on Whitehall Street." It was shot through with phrases like "a paradise for shoppers" and "manifold treasures."

"Atlanta's womankind has received a most wonderful New Year's gift," effused the writer, "and unlike most gifts this one will wear well, it will be becoming, it will please the artistic sense, cater to the gladsome fulness or distressful emptiness of the purse; it will always fit, being made after the latest pattern and finished by an artist's hand; it will spread light and good cheer in the pathway and best of all, it is something that vain humanity in general can point to with pride and call its own."

Having thus warmed up, the writer got to the point: "This wonderful gift is M. Rich & Bros. Co.'s new store—more familiarly known as 'Rich's,' which was thrown open to the public yesterday."

At that, there were some pretty stunning innovations in this store—plate glass show windows, elevators (consistently referred to as "giant elevators"), a skylight which gave the customer the advantage of being able to check her merchandise by daylight, as well as by electric light, a soda fountain, an employees' dining room, and a marvelously convenient loading area in the back where "a half dozen wagons may be loaded or unloaded at the same time." (It takes space for 150 trucks and station wagons now.)

So carried away was the reporter with the mahogany-paneled walls and shelves that he compared one wrapping counter to the pew of "ancient English churches," except for the cash register and telephone.

5

"COTTON AS CASH"

Walter Rich, son of Emanuel and nephew of Morris and Daniel, came home from Columbia University in 1901 to take his place in the store. He had worked as a stock boy during vacations but now he began an apprenticeship in the important yard goods department.

Within a short time young Walter progressed to the post of buyer and was making trips to the markets of the East and Europe, as his father had done. From the first, he reflected his family's enthusiasm for beautiful things and was bringing back Italian glass, Irish linens, lace from Brussels, delftware from The Hague.

Atlanta was ready for elegance. During the first decade of the new century the hills and forests and the old corn fields were being turned into homesites, some of them of considerable splendor. In May 1908 the newspapers heralded a "gigantic land sale," the 1492 Druid Hills acres belonging to Joel Hurt at "a cool half million—the largest sale ever recorded here." The purchasers were a syndicate headed by Asa G. Candler, the Coca-Cola man, Preston G. Arkwright, and Forrest and George Adair, who immediately began road building and installation of gas, electric, water, and sewer lines.

Ansley Park had been opened up by the sale in 1904 of

more than two hundred acres of land belonging to the estate
of George Washington Collier. This land had been owned by
but three persons since it was originally granted to Jonathon
Carroll in 1825. Carroll sold it in 1827 for fifty dollars and
in 1847 Collier bought it for $150. By 1904 the lots were
selling for an unprecedented sixty, seventy, and eighty dollars
a front foot.

City people began to buy country places out on West
Pace's Ferry Road, where Robert F. Maddox, the banker-
mayor, set the style by building a home on the land the state
was later to acquire for a Governor's Mansion.

Social clubs were being organized or were expanding. After
a fire which destroyed its clubhouse on Piedmont, the Gentlemen's Driving Club considered moving out but gave up the
idea and rebuilt on the old site. The Standard Club was
organized in 1905 with Walter H. Rich one of its founders
and its first treasurer. His associate at Rich's, David Strauss,
served as the first secretary.

There were so many "automobilists," as the society editors
called them, that Atlanta felt a need for a country club. The
Capital City Club downtown bought land at Brookhaven and
a hundred gentlemen, interested in the new game of golf,
launched the East Lake Country Club with a barbecue on the
spot and by subscribing five hundred dollars each.

Atlanta had its first automotive fatality of record. A
Marietta citizen lost control of his White Steamer, overturned
on a dirt road, and was killed. The city council met and
adopted an ordinance making eight miles an hour the speed
limit, except downtown where it was illegal to operate at a
speed "greater than a walk." Four or five years later the state
would take cognizance of this modern hazard and pass a
state law, requiring at least one white light throwing a beam
one hundred feet on automobiles driven between sunset and
sunrise. This law also made it mandatory for operators of
cars, when approaching a pedestrian, horse, or other draft

animals, to "give reasonable warning by use of a bell, horn, gong, or other signal."

Terminal station was completed in 1905 and opened with fanfare. J. W. English, the Confederate captain, bank president, and former mayor of Atlanta, was president of the terminal company and the proud dispatcher of the first message from the station's new Postal Telegraph and Cable Company. He sent it to Samuel Spencer, president of the Southern Railway in New York, saying: "The Atlanta Terminal station is now open to the public. The people of this section and those who enter Atlanta's gates owe you and the Central of Georgia and the Atlanta and West Point railroads an everlasting debt of gratitude."

After sending two more ceremonial messages to other officials, Captain English "threw aside his dignity," the newspapers reported, "and Panama hat in hand, led the Sixteenth Infantry band through the main entrance of the station, while the populace, gathered to witness the opening, cheered and applauded."

Special trains were coming every year or so, bringing such people as President Theodore Roosevelt, who made a trip to Roswell to visit the home of his mother, the former Miss Mittie (Martha) Bulloch; President-elect and Mrs. William Howard Taft, and a man who was to be President, New Jersey Governor Woodrow Wilson.

Ponce de Leon Park, long a recreation spot for Atlantans, was rebuilt and nearly every Sunday afternoon saw families and courting couples by the hundreds driving out to partake of this "phantasmagoria of countless attractions."

The municipal auditorium was opened and the Atlanta Music Festival Association, which enlisted the enthusiastic support of Walter Rich, planned a music festival for 1909, which was to be the forerunner of the city's Metropolitan Opera season. Enrico Caruso was the star of the two-day festival, backed up by a chorus of five hundred local singers and such imports as Geraldine Farrar and Giovanni Zenatello.

All of this growth, both physical and cultural, had its
impact on the mercantile business. Rich's stocked chic motor-
ing costumes for the ladies as well as opera finery.

In recognition of the growing interest in motor cars (thirteen hundred were owned by Atlantans in 1909), the town
celebrated "Automobile Week," and Asa Candler announced
the opening of the Atlanta Speedway out near Hapeville.
(This race-track, using three hundred acres of land, was to
become the nucleus of Atlanta's present airport.) Name
racers of the day, Arthur Chevrolet, Louis Strang, and Barney
Oldfield, set new records at the speedway and Rich's announced a noon closing "to enable our entire force to attend
the Speedway Races."

The Morris Richs were among the families to buy an
electric automobile. Their daughter, Mrs. Myers, recalls that
every time they drove out Peachtree Street, when they passed
the intersection of Peachtree and Ponce de Leon her mother
remarked that she would like to live there. It was a residential
corner then and the two-story frame house of Major Livingston Mims on the northeast corner had one of the prettiest
gardens in town. But in 1910 it came down to make way for
Joseph F. Gatin's new Georgian Terrace Hotel.

The hotel, which Rich's was to furnish, formally opened
in October 1911 with an estimated five thousand visitors
in attendance, bedazzling everybody and Mrs. Rich in particular. Her two daughters were grown up and married and
she saw no reason why she and Morris should maintain the
big house on Pryor Street. Shortly after that the Rich residential complex broke up.

Morris and Maud moved to an apartment in the Georgian
Terrace, where they were to live the remainder of their lives.
The Daniel Richs moved to Peachtree Circle in Ansley Park,
and Mrs. Emanuel Rich moved to Fairview Road in Druid
Hills. Walter, who was to marry Miss Marjory Myers of
Savannah in 1912, became the owner of a thirty-one-acre farm

in the heart of one of the city's most fashionable residential sections at 330 Argonne Drive.

Love of the land ran in the family, and young Walter inherited it in large measure. He said he took up farming because he was "the worst golfer in forty-eight states and two territories" and he did it in style—wearing bib overalls, a big straw hat, and plowing two mules named Chewing Gum and Madame Queen.

Because the South's economy was an agrarian economy the vicissitudes of the farmer were very real to the Richs. They were among the merchants and business leaders who met in the summer of 1914 to help find a remedy for the cotton emergency. When World War I broke out in Europe in August of 1914 Georgians felt it immediately. Their overseas markets for cotton were sealed off and all the major cotton exchanges in this country were closed. Bales of cotton were stacked high on the streets of many Georgia towns and in less than a month the price for middling cotton dropped from twelve cents a pound to six cents a pound. Among the remedies tried was a "Buy a Bale of Cotton" movement launched by a committee of one hundred leading business-men recruited by the Chamber of Commerce. One of the five who comprised the executive committee was David Strauss, Rich's financial chief.

Patriotic Atlantans rallied to the movement, buying a total of 301 bales at ten cents a pound (fifty dollars a bale), and Rich's was among the stores, hotels, and banks to decorate lobbies and windows with bales of cotton.

Walter Rich was to recall this in 1931 when the cotton market was again congested and Georgia farmers had cotton they couldn't dispose of. Rich's would take up to five thousand bales in exchange for merchandise, allowing a premium of one cent a pound over the market price, he announced.

"This will not be the first time that Rich's has bought cotton to help the farmer," he said in an interview with the Atlanta *Georgian*. "In 1914 when the beginning of the

World War brought on grave industrial problems, Rich's accepted cotton at above the market price, in exchange for merchandise."

When things got rough in 1931 cotton farmers remembered Rich's and wrote "Mr. Walter."

He knew the old plight too well. Farmers had cotton and they had food. But there was no cash for clothes for the family, for sweaters and school shoes and books.

Rich's, he told them, would gladly accept "cotton as cash" and not count it altruism but sound business practice, "as the South is sound, strong as the economic foundation of Georgia and helpful only as it is the duty and privilege of every worthy institution to be in a period of difficulty and adjustments."

He summed up the situation: "You know Atlanta and Rich's are so bound together, so united, so part and parcel of my mental picture that it is very nearly impossible for me to regard one without the other.

"All my life I have been a part of Rich's, and all my life Rich's has been bone and sinew of the civic and economic life of Atlanta. Today, as always, with me the two are merged. We of Rich's simply regard this merchandise for cotton plan as our bit in the present difficulty. If it is as helpful as we are certain it will be, this Southern institution will proudly add another service stripe to those we've earned previously in our sixty-four years of campaigning as good soldiers in the cause of Atlanta, Georgia, and the entire South."

As a result of the 1914 cotton crisis, Atlanta's wealthiest citizen, Asa Candler, built the enormous Candler warehouse on a forty-acre tract known as the Anthony Murphy property in West End. During the first two weeks it was open in 1915 it received an average of one thousand bales of cotton a day, upon which the Central Bank & Trust Corporation, of which Mr. Candler was president, loaned an average of one hundred thousand dollars per day.

The warehouse was to serve the government as a quarter-master depot during both World Wars I and II and today is Rich's major warehouse facility, where the store uses a total of 450,000 square feet.

Walter Rich was elected vice president of Rich's in 1920, a post he held until 1926, when he succeeded his Uncle Morris as president. Morris, then seventy-nine years old, was named chairman of the board.

The store had started outgrowing its new Whitehall Street building almost the day it opened, and negotiations were soon started for a new site. A fifty-two-year lease was taken on a 200×120 foot lot at the corner of Alabama and Broad streets, a transaction which Forrest Adair, the realtor handling the deal, said would aggregate $4,242,000 in rentals—the biggest deal of its kind in the history of the community.

The new store, extravagantly dubbed "Rich's Palace of Commerce" by the newspapers, opened Monday, March 24, 1924. A series of parties and promotions followed, with Morris himself giving the final one in May with a luncheon for fifty-seven friends who were fifty-seven years old.

In an interview shortly before the move from Whitehall Street, Morris discussed the years there and reminisced about the old days when wagon yards spilled out country people come to town to trade. It was not uncommon, he said, to see a customer take a piece of material, ravel out the edge, and chew the thread to see if it was pure wool. Another test was to set fire to a small scrap of material and sniff the smoke.

When they paid their bills farmers expected a lagniappe, some small thing like a spool of thread or a trifle for the children to be "thrown in."

Morris was eighty-one years old and the new store but four when he died. He was stricken with a heart attack while he and Mrs. Rich were vacationing in Atlantic City, June 29, 1928. His daughter, Rosalind, and his grandson, Richard, were at his bedside when death came. The funeral was held in

Atlanta with his nephews serving as pallbearers, and he was buried in old Oakland Cemetery near Emanuel and Daniel and not too far from his parents, Joseph and Rose.

Later Myrta Lockett Avary, the author of several books about the Civil War period, was to write Morris's family of one of the many quiet, unrecorded kindnesses he did. She knew a man, a schoolteacher, who was in bad health and unable to work. His wife was terribly worried about providing for their several school-age children and she was feeling keenly the pressure of their unpaid bills, particularly one at Rich's.

"She was a lady of fine pride," wrote Mrs. Avary. "It was a hard thing for her to do when she went to Mr. Rich and told him she was unable to pay the bill already due; and then about the children and their needs. 'It was the hardest thing I ever did,' she said. 'And the worst of it was that I could see no certain way in which I could pay. I told him the situation and broke down—not crying but subsiding into silence and humiliation.'"

Morris smiled at her gently, the woman related, and said, "Don't give yourself any trouble about this bill. I know you'll pay it when you can." And then with a humorous glint in his brown eyes back of the pince-nez he added, "One of these children will pay it with interest if we have to wait."

He told her to buy whatever she needed in his store on her charge account, "comforted her about her husband's health and sent her forth 'with my courage and self-respect recovered,'" Mrs. Avary related. "It was this that helped her as much, if not more, than the money indulgence."

The author said she personally remembered Mr. Morris riding around "in a little electric . . . with that beautiful white head, the head of an aristocrat."

She added: "The world is so full of the painful and un-pleasant that it is a pleasure and help for me to remember in my isolation and illness things of beauty and kindliness that have bloomed and may still be blooming in our world of war and sadness."

John K. Ottley, president of the Fourth National Bank
(later to merge with the First National), who knew him for
forty years, wrote Mrs. Rich of "that brave immigrant boy
at the very foot of the ladder, alone in an alien land."

"Fortunate it was that he came to Atlanta—not for him,
I mean, for the success he merited would have come to him
anywhere; but for us. Think of Atlanta then, without the
contribution to its commercial life, the impress upon its civic
progress and well-being, made through sixty years by Morris
Rich."

The newspapers spoke of his appreciation of music and his
support of efforts to "make the best available to the public."
He was eighty-one years old, they noted, "and no Atlantan
ever crowded his years with more useful service."

6

ENTER AN ENGINEER

"As frequently happens when a person, a nation, or a business is presented with great need, someone comes along with a solution which opens dozens of new doors in seemingly impregnable walls."

Frank H. Neely, who wrote that in his book, *The Manager: A Human Engineer*, might have been speaking of himself. For when he came along to Rich's in 1924 the store was, in truth, "presented with a great need."

Morris had lost his brothers, Emanuel in 1897 and Daniel in 1920, and he was himself an old man, seventy-seven years old. Lucian York, general manager of the store for thirteen years, had died suddenly of a heart attack. Walter Rich, Emanuel's son and a vice president, found himself with a new $1,500,000 building on Broad and Alabama streets, a part of town the experts were saying was dead. Fresh and formidable competition was coming in with the announcement from New York that Macy's was buying out Davison-Paxon, a big new store in the "better" part of town on Peachtree Street. Business was good but not good enough.

Walter Rich knew Mr. and Mrs. Frank Neely socially. Mrs. Neely, the former Rae Schlesinger, a graduate of Smith, had been teaching the Richs' daughter, Bee, along with their own daughter, Rachel, at home and the families were good friends of long standing.

Mr. Rich was among many southern businessmen who had been impressed by the novel achievements of forty-year-old Frank Neely, an engineer, in such seemingly unrelated fields as the Schlesingers' candy factory, Fulton Bag and Cotton Mills, and Westinghouse Electric in Pittsburgh. What Mr. Neely had done to step up production and streamline the operations of these enterprises he might do at Rich's.

Mr. Neely demurred. He didn't know anything about department stores, he said. But Walter Rich and his chief of financial matters, David H. Strauss, persisted.

Finally, to settle the subject, Mr. Neely mentioned what he considered would be a prohibitive salary, a figure five thousand dollars a year more than he was making at the Fulton Bag and Cotton Mills.

"When can you come to work?" Walter Rich asked.

As Tom Mahoney wrote in *The Saturday Evening Post* in 1949, "Thus it came about that Rich's is the only department store in the nation which has been run for quarter of a century by an engineer."

Frank Neely at the age of eighty-three is still there, an active, influential chairman of the store's executive committee. His list of achievements and honors, not only in the vineyard of Rich's itself but in the affairs of the city and state, grows longer with each passing year and new honors come to him regularly.

The son of a Confederate veteran and the youngest of nine children, young Frank Neely was born in Augusta, Georgia, in 1884 and grew up in Floyd County in northwest Georgia. His mother's people were the famous Longstreets, authors, educators, and inventors. His father, who had run away to sea as a boy and come home the master of five languages, served in the Confederate intelligence service. After the war he led in establishing the public school systems of Richmond and Floyd counties. Neely High School in Rome, Georgia, is named for him.

After his father's death relatives took a hand in rearing

young Frank and, to the surprise of his education-minded family, he was not particularly enthusiastic about school, particularly the study of Latin. It wasn't until he saw a piece of new farm machinery demonstrated on a nearby farm that he began to take seriously the importance of education. He went home and told his aunt that he was going to study hard, go to Georgia Tech, and become an engineer.

At the age of sixteen he was well on the way. He took two steps which were to profoundly influence his life. After a summer of hard study he passed the entrance requirement and was accepted as a freshman at Tech and he met the girl who was to become his wife. Some fellow students took him to call on Rae Schlesinger and he made a favorable impression on this bright and popular young woman immediately. He was the only boy present who stood up the whole time her mother was in the room.

Eight years later they were married at what Mrs. Neely remembers as "a grand wedding" in the Schlesinger home. They went to live in Pittsburgh where Frank was working for Westinghouse.

In Pittsburgh young Frank had discovered the writings and teachings of Frederick Taylor and Henry L. Gantt on scientific management and was so attracted by their theories that he asked for a transfer to plant operations, where he could work under Gantt, who was a consulting engineer. When he and Mrs. Neely came back to Atlanta in 1910 he had learned much of the production and management methods which he hoped to use in the South, where industrialization was young and management skills scarce.

Back home his first job was in his father-in-law's candy factory, which he rebuilt, putting in scientific management and a method of cooling and wrapping candy. His next was as director of production of the Fulton Bag and Cotton Mills, which operated six plants in as many states. His application of the Gantt "task and bonus" method was the first in the textile industry. By this time he was one of Gantt's favorite pupils and was often in the famed engineer's home on his trips to New York.

With that background, Frank Neely came to Rich's. And things started popping.

As Mr. Neely now recalls, the new six-story store was fine "but still a country store." He brought in New York designers and lighting experts to redesign showcases and flood the entire store with light. He instituted a method of inventory and stock control, which seemed elementary to the merchants after they got the hang of it, but which was unheard of at the time. Rich's buyers have always had a fairly free hand when they go to market but Mr. Neely thought it was time to tighten the reins in 1924 when one buyer went off to New York with thirty thousand dollars to buy men's furnishings and came home instead with a deed to a South Georgia hosiery mill.

Both mill and buyer were speedily jettisoned.

One of Mr. Neely's most notable firsts was the installation of air conditioning in Rich's, the first store in the country to be completely air-conditioned.

"Windows had to be open to let in air," he recalls. "The railroad tracks were close and steam engines were passing all the time, belching out smoke and showering the merchandise with soot. I had used air conditioning at the candy factory to cool the candy and I thought we could work out a system here."

York, the air-conditioning firm, was pleased to work with Mr. Neely but a little skeptical because they had not perfected a method of cooling a place where there would be a constant stream of people coming in from the outside, bringing body heat and the heat of the southern sun in their clothes. Together Mr. Neely and York worked out a system which he now says was "the damndest abortion you ever saw from an engineering point of view." But it worked in 1926 and it is still working in the main store today.

The fact that they didn't know for sure what they had is

Famous Rich's clock at the corner of Broad and Alabama Streets, a symbol of the store and a favorite meeting place for Atlantans.

Artist's conception of Morris Rich's original store, which opened on Whitehall Street in 1867.

A bill of goods receipt from Rich's, 1886.

Portrait of founder Morris Rich.

1887 Rich's advertisement from *The Atlanta Constitution.*

Customers and employees gather at 54-56 Whitehall Street, January 1907, for the gala opening of the "new" Rich's.

Rich's annual Harvest Sale, from the 1950s.

Early 1930s street scene of Rich's at the corner of Broad and Alabama Streets.

Steinway used by Paderewski on his 1892–93 concert tour, shown with Verne Manley, Director of Rich's Music Center. The piano graced the music center for years.

Mary Hendricks puts finishing touches on one of Rich's legendary wedding cakes.

photo courtesy *The Atlanta Journal-Constitution*

Generations of children have been thrilled by riding Rich's Pink Pig.

photo courtesy *The Atlanta Journal-Constitution*

"Oldsters" reunion in 1980, where Annie Duffey Moseley, 104, and Will Tench, 108, are honored as the oldest customers at the Rich's annual 80-Year-Party.

Lighting of the Great Tree, a time-honored Rich's tradition.

evidenced by Rich's introduction of the cooling system without any fanfare.

"We did it quietly," says Mr. Neely, "because we didn't know if it would work."

Happiest among the employees when the windows were sealed and the soot no longer flew was Mrs. Rose Kling, who could then keep pristine clean her stock of underwear, corsets and, as Mr. Neely wryly puts it, "what she *would* call 'intimate apparel.'"

The land the new store stood on had been secured by long-term lease, mostly from the family of the pioneer settler, Capt. J. W. English. Mr. Neely began work almost at once to buy that land and other parcels adjoining it for possible future expansion. He foresaw a time when Rich's would need more extensive warehouse and loading facilities, and he launched the slow, trouble-fraught task of acquiring a lot at a time. A twelve-foot strip along what is now the Hunter Street viaduct gave him the most trouble. It was occupied mostly by small merchants and some of it was involved in family squabbles and litigation. One particular plot was a thorn in his flesh for nearly twenty years.

"I learned at the tax office that it was owned by two women who lived in New York," he remembers. "I wrote them but they wouldn't answer my letters."

That went on for years until Mr. Neely learned by chance the name of a New York real estate man who had had dealings with them. He started working with him, trying to find his way through a family feud involving cats and church. It seems that the women lived together and owned a lot of land together and could agree about nothing. One of them feared that the other was going to give everything they owned to her church. The other was certain the less religious sister was going to give everything to a cat hospital. Mr. Neely finally worked out a lease arrangement with them which terminated in a sale when they both died. He doesn't know whether church or cats got the rest of their land.

Perhaps more far-reaching in effect than even the air conditioning, which stores throughout the country would eventually copy, was the Neely-initiated system of letting the customer make her own adjustment.

"The first thing I did was to abolish the adjustment bureau," he remembers. "We advertised that henceforth the customer would make her own adjustment. A woman who had not been in Rich's for years came to see me and asked if we meant what we said."

She had spent four hundred dollars for a rug which had not worn well and when she spoke to the man in the adjustment bureau about it he had asked how many dogs she had in the house. The affronted customer had turned on her heel and left the store, never to return—until she saw the ad about the customer-adjustment policy.

Mr. Neely gave her a check for four hundred dollars and the store's sincere apologies. She and her children and grandchildren have been firm Rich's friends since.

"She didn't want to take the whole amount," says Mr. Neely, "but I wouldn't let her leave without it. People will be much more liberal if you let them decide what's fair."

Not all employees were jubilant over this turn of events. Among the skeptics was R. B. Eason, the now retired transportation expert who was doing a stint in the repair department at the time.

Electric refrigerators, those memorable first ones with the motor in a sort of cupola on top, were just out and Rich's was selling its with a five-year guarantee. A customer had one a few months and complained to Mr. Eason that the exterior paint was flaking off. She wanted it repainted.

"I was trying to economize in my department and win a Stetson hat," Mr. Eason says. "I told her it was the operation of the refrigerator and not the paint job that was guaranteed for five years."

The customer called Mr. Neely and Mr. Neely called Mr.

Eason. Within a couple of hours the refrigerator was in Rich's big basement workroom being repainted.

"The next time Mr. Neely passed this way and stuck his head in the door I jumped him about it," says Mr. Eason. "I felt like I was right and I sure hated to lose that Stetson hat. I never had had one. He told me it's the customer that's *always* right and he wasn't kidding. He said people don't like to have their mistakes pointed out to them, especially customers."

Mr. Eason took that homily so to heart that when a newly married couple called up and asked him to send out and oil the springs in a brand-new innerspring mattress, which was squeaking, he didn't argue. He told the repairman to investigate the possibility that the slats were not arranged properly "but be sure and have an oilcan in your hand when you go in there."

This Rich's policy became famous fast—and Rich's hastened the fame by mentioning it frequently in a series of institutional ads, which Mr. Neely inaugurated. He felt then that Rich's could not hope to buy more space than the other stores (it soon would), but he felt a distinctive use of the space they did buy would have a telling effect. He started a Monday morning institutional ad in the *Constitution*, which has run for more than thirty years, won prizes, imitators, and the attention of readers all over the country.

Through the years that series has stated and restated nine points about Rich's: 1. The customer is always right. 2. The customer makes her own adjustment. 3. Quality for quality, Rich's will never be undersold. 4. Rich's creates low prices. 5. Liberal credit. 6. Rich's, the one-stop store. 7. Rich's community shopping center. 8. Atlanta born, Atlanta owned, Atlanta managed. 9. A Southern institution since 1867.

While making these points Rich's has at the same time identified with the past of the state in a series on history, supported civic and philanthropic endeavor with ads saluting schools or colleges or plugging for the PTA, the Easter seal,

or some similar campaign. Sometimes the ads are hardly
ads at all but expressions of Rich's kinship with the city, as
in the use of the 23rd Psalm the day after the Paris air-
plane crash. Sometimes they are poignant, making a plea
for support for the United Appeal. Sometimes they make a
whimsical pitch for some store policy, as in the widely copied
ad showing a measles-spattered little boy who wished his
mother had got his measles at Rich's "so we could take them
back."

While revamping the looks of the store and shoring up
some of its policies regarding the customer, Mr. Neely put in
practice his theories calling for definite standards for workers,
training them to meet those standards and compensating them
well. The quota bonus plan, a free clinic, a credit union,
insurance and pensions for all employees, all were started
during the Neely regime and ahead of other stores in the
region. This was a Gantt precept—good working conditions,
good employee relations—and there was another which Mr.
Neely was already disposed to take to heart: Participation in
the civil life of the community.

In 1926 he was named Atlanta's "Citizen of the Year" for
his service as chairman of the Atlanta bond commission,
which supervised the construction of ten million dollars' worth
of viaduct construction, a new city hall, schools, and made
basic surveys for the present sewer system. He was an or-
ganizer and first chairman of the Georgia State Department
of Commerce and served on several commissions of Presidents, among them President Kennedy's White House Committee on Youth Employment.

During the World War II years, when all the young men
in the store, including Dick Rich, were in the service, Frank
Neely and Walter Rich ran the store and served the war
effort at home.

Director and chairman of the Federal Reserve Bank of
Atlanta for sixteen years, Mr. Neely was also regional director
of the War Production Board and instrumental in bringing

Lockheed's forerunner, the Bell Aircraft Corporation, to Atlanta. He was first chairman of the Georgia Nuclear Advisory Commission and instrumental in the construction of a nuclear research reactor at Georgia Tech and the establishment of the School of Nuclear Engineering there—both done with funds from The Rich Foundation. In recognition of his service in this area Tech recently named the school "The Frank H. Neely Nuclear Center."

Georgia Tech, to which he aspired in his youth, has continued to hold a priority on his affections. But Mr. Neely, basically a restless, inquiring mind, has many interests. He turned three hundred acres of eroded Georgia farmland into a showplace on the Chattahoochee, building up a Guernsey dairy herd of such impeccable standards he went to court back in the early 1940's to fight a pasteurization ordinance. The health officials, who wanted mandatory pasteurization for all milk sold in Atlanta, won. The Neelys now sell their raw milk wholesale, but visitors to their farm or to their apartment at the Biltmore Hotel are often served thick sweet cream in its raw state with their tea or coffee.

As John A. Sibley, prominent Atlanta banker and civic leader, said when he introduced Mr. Neely to the Newcomen Society to make a speech a few years ago, there never is time to enumerate the honors Frank Neely has won. A modest man, he does not dwell on them himself but he can't help being proud of two of them—the Henry Laurence Gantt Memorial Gold Medal, presented jointly by the American Society of Mechanical Engineers and the American Management Association, and the Frederick W. Taylor Key Award for his "creative and imaginative" approach in business and education, his "untiring efforts" in behalf of his city, state, and nation, and his "stimulating leadership" in the improvement of schools.

7

THE FAMILY CONTINUES

When Dick Rich came home from running Rich's New York office in 1935 to take his first executive job in the store, that of advertising director, they assigned him a young secretary practically straight out of Commercial High School, seventeen-year-old Dorothy Weiner.

Timorous but determined to start off right, Dorothy began by straightening up her new boss's desk and taking up a handsome crystal inkwell encrusted in filigreed brass, which had belonged to his grandfather, and filling it with ink in the ubiquitous Rich's shade of green.

Shaking a little from nervousness and fear that she would drop the heirloom, the girl carefully bore the inkwell to her employer's desk and set it down with a final triumphant flourish.

Dick Rich gazed at it thoughtfully for a moment and then gave her one of his typical quiet, eye-crinkling smiles.

"Thank you, Dorothy," he said, "but you shouldn't have bothered. We don't keep ink in my grandfather's inkwell any more. We've stopped using quill pens."

It was, in a way, a statement of policy. A new generation had arrived in Morris's old store and with it new ideas, new methods, and the fresh venturesomeness and enthusiasm of youth.

The old inkwell, along with the rest of the ornate set, is

still on Dick Rich's desk, the same graceful, old-time double desk which belonged to his grandfather. One side of the desk is against the wall now but he remembers when first his Uncle Daniel used it and then his grandmother, driving to town to pick up Morris, used to sit there opposite her husband and write notes to their grandchildren.

Until a few years ago when it finally gave out, he sat in his grandfather's swivel chair. There is a silver framed picture of Morris on the desk, and on the wall to the right of it pictures of his own family—his late wife, the beautiful former Virginia Lazarus of New Orleans, who died in 1957, their daughters Sally (Mrs. William Rose) and Virginia (Mrs. Robert Barnett), their son, Michael, and eight assorted grandchildren. The other furniture in the room, a plain table with a glass top, worn leather chairs and divan, is old and comfortable and unpretentious.

The office, employees say, reflects the same simplicity of taste that was Morris Rich's. "Mr. Dick," they say, is very like his grandfather in appearance, in manner and, except for a slight trace of distinctive coastal Savannah accent, in his speech. This may be a fond conceit of people who take pride in the fact that Rich's is a "family" enterprise, for these same people see in their "Mr. Dick's" son, Michael, a buyer in the Budget Store, a marked resemblance to young Richard Rich at his age.

Whether or not it is true, the fact is that Richard H. Rich has had to run a store in a very different world than either his grandfather or his older cousin, Walter, knew. While Morris worried that he couldn't be close to eight hundred employees, Dick works hard to stay in touch with thousands. In his day Walter Rich called himself "the eternal floorwalker" and was famous for visiting each department and speaking to each sales person every day. Dick Rich through a determined decentralization of authority depends upon seven other top executives to keep him abreast of happenings throughout the main store and its five branches.

It's a computer age and Rich's has a floor full of them scientifically totting up transactions and clattering out bills. But kindergarteners, thanking Mr. Rich for a party or an art show, still crayon hearts and flowers on their rough tablet paper and sign themselves, "Love, Debbie" and "Love, Paul." And Dick Rich personally pins orchids and gold pins on employees who attain coveted membership in the twenty-year and forty-year clubs.

As Morris's first male heir, young Dick was probably destined from earliest childhood to take a hand in running the store. Born in Atlanta December 24, 1901, he was always a favorite with his grandfather. He started during vacations, when he was a teen-age boy, coming up from his parents' home in Savannah to stay with his grandparents and work, first as a bundle wrapper and then as a stock boy and later as a salesman.

Conscientious from the first, the boy would not leave at the end of the day until he had his work done and they say at Rich's that many a time the venerable, white-haired president, Morris, would be found helping young Dick finish his packages so they could walk home together.

When he was graduated from the University of Pennsylvania in 1923 with a Bachelor of Science degree in economics, the family began to make serious plans for his future in the store. It was Walter Rich's idea that he take his mother's maiden name of Rich, if he were ever to head the enterprise of the same name—and his parents, Herman and Rosalind Rosenheim, agreed. (Mr. and Mrs. Rosenheim died within two days of each other in 1961.)

And so young Richard Rosenheim became Richard H. Rich.

He went to Harvard for graduate courses and entered an extended internship, which involved working in silk mills in New Jersey to learn about fabrics, the garment district of New York City to study production methods, L. Bamberger & Co., the mercantile concern of Newark, N.J., and Europe for a

time, where he went with his cousin, Walter, to acquaint him-
self with Rich's foreign resources. He spent a year in the New
York office before coming home, bringing with him the lovely
Virginia, to whom he was married in 1930.

A further apprenticeship awaited him at home. The team
of Walter Rich, Frank Neely, and David Strauss was still
very much in command of the store and they were committed
to the proposition that even if you were named Rich, you
had to earn your way upward in the store. Young Dick set to
work in advertising and public relations and had worked himself up to the post of vice president when World War II broke
out. One of his early civic assignments was that of civilian
adviser to the Secretary of the Army, providing liaison between the military and good potential officer candidates in the
southeastern states. So enthusiastic did he become about the
service, as he helped screen other men for it, that he enlisted
himself in the Air Force.

After three years in the service, ending up in Brazil, where
he was special assistant to the U. S. Ambassador, Major Rich
came home. David Strauss had died in 1936 and the post of
vice president and treasurer fell to him.

There were many changes and, in spite of war shortages,
some expansion. Rich's became a member of the Associated
Merchandising Corporation in 1943. AMC is a service organization owned and managed by its twenty-five members,
some of the finest individually owned stores in America.

The Rich Foundation was established to distribute a large
share of the profits of the store to the Atlanta community.
The first large gift was one of $250,000 for a business school
building at Emory University to honor the founders of Rich's,
Morris, Emanuel, and Daniel, and $100,000 to strengthen the
teaching staff. The foundation would later donate a radio
station to the city and county school systems, the computer
center at Georgia Tech, an out-patient ward to Georgia
Baptist Hospital, a laboratory for the industrial engineering

department of Georgia Tech, and a wing at St. Joseph's Infirmary, as well as many smaller contributions to drives and campaigns.

On August 21, 1945 Rich's held a victory staff meeting to make preparations for welcoming back its own—Rich's employees who had gone to war. Those who were killed in line of duty would be memorialized, their names inscribed on a bronze plaque and a war bond sent to the charitable institution or church selected by their parents or wives.

"And now the living veterans will return to us from time to time, as they are released," Mr. Walter told the meeting. "We will go beyond our pledge to Uncle Sam—the return of their jobs for at least one year—and here is where you and I can be of great value in making their future a happy, successful one. The war was a shock to these men and women. There is a problem in the return from military to civil or business activities. Many flounder and stumble. Let each and every one of you be their prop. Let us welcome them with our hearts and our hands. . . . Do not let us stop with the promise I gave each man and woman, to look after their dear ones in case of emergency during their absence. Let us carry on with the heroes when they return."

Walter Rich, widely respected in the community and genuinely loved in the store, received many awards in his lifetime but one of the most prized came the last year of his life. This was the Tobe Award, a crystal plaque set on an ebony base, presented to him in New York in January 1947 for "distinguished contributions to American retailing." Dorothy Shaver, president of Lord & Taylor, said Mr. Rich was honored not so much for his undeniable success in merchandising but because he was a merchant who realized "that human values are paramount," recognized his obligation to the community at large, and was "sensitive to the attitudes of the people with whom he works and with those of the customers with whom he deals."

Mr. Rich died the following November, mourned by people

throughout the region. He had, like his Uncle Morris, been kind to many people in ways that nobody else knew about. A member of the Hebrew Benevolent Congregation, he nonetheless supported churches, schools, and hospitals no matter the denomination. He served on the Fulton-DeKalb Hospital Authority, which operates the big charity hospital named for Henry Grady, and he was a valued member of the executive committee of St. Joseph's Infirmary, where in memory of his mother he designated 150 shares of Rich's stock to be used in support of the free clinic. He was an enthusiastic supporter of the little Methodist school, Young Harris College, in the mountains of North Georgia, giving funds for a farm school and home economics building.

Of the many tributes which came from people all over the country, the governor, the mayor, and newspaper editors, the one from Rich's employees would have pleased Mr. Walter most.

He was, one of them wrote in a little "In Memoriam" booklet which was published later, "a genius in sensing the trend of the market and the wishes of his customers."

"But his was an even greater gift for getting along with people. He loved people, and he especially loved those at Rich's, four thousand strong in 1947. He was our staunch friend (and sometimes severest critic). To us he was simply 'Mr. Walter.' We depended on him for help in our troubles, for inspiration, for guidance. We went to his office at any time of the day, to ask his advice or help. We were never made to wait; we were never turned away. . . . He set standards for his personnel that were sometimes hard to live up to. But he provided us with every convenience, every comfort, every measure for our security. Our well-being was always his first concern. He provided hospitalization and insurance, a clinic, a recreation roof, lounges, a cafeteria where we might eat amid pleasant surroundings at prices just above cost; he fostered hobby groups and team sports, in pursuit of which we could come to know one another. He was instrumental in organizing an employees' credit union. When there were deaths in our families we received flowers with his card and a note of sympathy. On our store anniversaries, we were remembered with candy or corsages or small gifts. When there were new babies in our families, Mr. Walter's personal check opened a bank account for the child's educational fund. . . . He leaves behind in all our hearts a great love for this kind, modest man. We will not forget him."

Following the death of Mr. Walter, Mr. Neely moved up to president, a post he held until 1949 when he became chairman of the board. In 1961 Harold Brockey became the fifth president of Rich's, Richard Rich became the third chairman of the board, and Mr. Neely became chairman of the seven-man Executive committee. This committee, which meets once a week, includes: Mr. Neely, Mr. Rich, Mr. Brockey, Vice Presidents Louis Carrol, Joseph F. Asher, Alvin Ferst, and Kenneth P. Mages, who is also treasurer.

The biggest building program in the store's history would be launched during Dick Rich's regime as president. The six-story Store for Men, presided over by Mr. Asher, was added in 1951; a new service building in 1958, and the first branch store, in the Lenox Shopping Center, in 1959. Lenox out Peachtree Road was an innovation for Atlanta with its bountiful parking in an area planted to flowering crabapple trees, its mall and fountains. Rich's, operating on four levels, was rapidly to get a new-looking customer, the northside housewife in shorts or pedal pushers. In 1959 the second branch was opened in the Belvedere Shopping Center, in 1963 a third in the new forty-two-acre Cobb County Shopping Center, in 1965 a fourth in the covered-mall-completely-air-conditioned North DeKalb Shopping Center, and also in 1965 a fifth in southwestern Atlanta at the new Greenbriar Shopping Center.

With the opening of each new branch store, there was

always the possibility that the downtown store would lose customers. On the contrary, business has kept pace with each expansion.

More than thirty years have passed since young Richard Rich came home from New York to sit at his grandfather's desk. The timid girl who started as his secretary was married during the war and widowed by the war. Except for a year when she was with her husband before he was sent off to Europe, Dorothy Weiner Lavine has been at Rich's. And except for the three years after he enlisted in the Air Force, she has been outside Dick Rich's door, cheerfully answering phone calls, mail, complaints, compliments, and a myriad of zany requests.

Awards have come to him in coveys, and sometimes Dorothy wages fruitless battle to decorate his office with plaques, cups, and framed certificates of various kinds. He allowed her to hang his certificate as civilian aide to the Secretary of the Army (this next to a photograph of him with President Lyndon B. Johnson). She also posted the National Retail Merchants' Association gold medal given him as the outstanding retailer in the United States. But the display of most honors embarrasses him.

To a secretary an employer often takes on heroic proportions. Mrs. Lavine knows Dick Rich as a man important in the business, civic, and artistic life of the region, but what she perhaps values most in him is the fact that he is a gentleman in the old-fashioned definition, which connotes patience, courtesy, fairness, and kindness to everybody.

At sixty-five he is trim, athletic, suntanned, playing tennis and swimming in his backyard every morning the weather permits. He is also a hard worker who seldom gets to the store later than 8:45 A.M., and is often downtown at meetings, business and civic, far, far into the night.

The list of organizations he works for as chairman, director, or trustee runs to thirty or forty. But he seems to have unlimited time for any random caller, whether it be governor or mayor wanting to talk about the Atlanta Rapid Transit Authority, which Mr. Rich heads, an employee with a grievance, or a child selling tickets to the Halloween carnival.

Mr. Rich himself gives credit for the time and attention he has for extra-store enterprises to his luck in having such able people as Harold Brockey running the store.

Mr. Brockey came up through the department store ranks, starting with Macy's training squad in New York. A genial, family-loving man (he is married to the former Claire Green of New York and they have two daughters and five grandchildren), Mr. Brockey follows the Rich's tradition of service in civic and philanthropic enterprises.

But the major portion of these good works falls on Dick Rich. The construction of a new art center, an endeavor which he has led, would have pleased Morris, Daniel, and especially Emanuel, "the artistic one." But the building of a new rapid transit system to ease Atlanta's traffic problems and transport workers and shoppers to the central city with lightning speed would probably be a marvel beyond comprehension.

They knew Atlanta *when*—when the possession of even a balky mule was marvelous transportation, and if a man had come home from the war with his own two legs strong and intact, he had "rapid transit" enough.

8

SPACE AGE MANAGEMENT

Morris Rich, who lucked into the little rough pine store building on Whitehall Street in 1867, taking it quickly and gladly because there weren't many buildings of any kind in Atlanta then, might have trouble understanding the way the space age management of his store operates.

Morris had to depend a lot on luck and guesswork. And although luck and guesswork undoubtedly are still ingredients in the decisions and big planning that go on at Rich's today, they represent a dash and a pinch in an awesomely scientific operation.

Morris opened his store on Whitehall Street because that was where he *could* open it. He ran it as best he knew how and, because he and his brothers were intelligent and diligent and had a few things working for them, such as a growing city, it panned out.

Today Morris's grandson no more relies solely on his own strengths and lucky happenstance than he sells fifty-cent corsets and high button shoes.

Dick Rich cannot emphasize enough the importance of the expertise of the men who, as he says, "really run the store." Nor does he forget their lieutenants, well-educated, precisely trained young men from universities and colleges throughout the country who harness and drive with consummate skill the modern merchant's work animals—computers, surveys, and all the machinery of scientific planning and engineering.

As president, Harold Brockey is the front line commander-in-chief of a colorful, volatile, astonishingly talented lineup. Mr. Rich describes him as a man of "dynamic drive, human attributes, great ability to evaluate and judge people and to motivate and inspire them."

Mr. Brockey joined Rich's in 1950 as general merchandise manager of the Store for Homes. He was named a director in 1953 and two years later became senior vice president and general merchandise manager of the entire store before taking on the job of executive vice president and general manager. In 1961 he became Rich's fifth president in its hundred-year history, the second person outside the Rich family to head the operation. Frank Neely was the first.

Although, like Mr. Neely, Mr. Brockey did not set out in life with a department store career in mind, his direction of Rich's has amazed the experts throughout the country and awed the home folks, including some of the old-timers in the store. During his administration Rich's has seen a period of almost phenomenal growth, including the opening of two new stores in one year. In the trade this feat is called fantastic. While business has advanced on all fronts, the sparkle and dash which its customers have come to expect of the old store has also progressed.

His associates say this is due mostly to the fact that Harold Brockey is both an imaginative man, who can "throw out a million ideas in a matter of minutes," and a solid administrator with prodigious memory for what has been done in the past and almost a seismic sensitivity to what the customer will be thinking about and wanting tomorrow.

The enormously popular home shows, now a twice-a-year event at Rich's, are an example of one Brockey idea that caught fire. Originating in the downtown Store for Homes and spreading out to the branch stores, these shows draw thousands of visitors from all parts of the country, most of whom say that they came to see what's new, to borrow ideas for use in their own homes, to be diverted by the bright and original touches of Rich's crack decorating staff. The fact that before they go home most of them have bought new furniture or old, oil paintings, table settings, new draperies, or new floor coverings is, of course, something Harold Brockey knew all the time would happen.

Mr. Brockey's consuming passion for knowledge was really the thing that led him to the retail business. Born in Chatham, N.J., one of five children, he was in Columbia University, readying himself to study medicine, when the depression of the 1930's hit. The study of medicine suddenly became an impossible luxury to a boy who had worked hard and helped out at home since his earliest youth. But Harold Brockey is in no sense a "dropout." Instead of continuing his education at Columbia, he simply switched schools. He joined Macy's executive training program.

A big department store, as all veteran retailers will tell you, is in many ways comparable to a university in its opportunities for learning. And young Mr. Brockey neglected none of them. An omnivorous reader, an insatiable seeker after knowledge, he worked hard and advanced rapidly, becoming a nationally recognized expert on home furnishings prior to his coming to Rich's.

Since the day a railroad man drove a stake in the ground and thereby picked the site for the future city of Atlanta, the town has been receptive to newcomers, new ideas, fresh energy. It didn't take the city long to recognize in Harold Brockey that it had a gold mine of ideas and energy.

In 1964 he headed the Community Chest drive, known locally as the United Appeal, and it swept over its quota for the first time in decades. His method was the same one he uses in the operation of Rich's: Pick able assistants and inspire them.

Eugene Patterson, editor of the *Constitution*, was so impressed by the Brockey approach to the United Appeal that he devoted his editorial page column to it.

"Harold Brockey said some things the other day that bear repeating," he wrote. "They concern the place of good intentions in our system of competitive enterprise. Karl Marx thought capitalism, being materially oriented, would wreck itself with selfishness. Arrayed against the law of help-yourself, however, are tempering forces rooted in religious belief.

"Religious and ethical beliefs have to be translated from Sunday morning into the working week, though, or Marx was right. And Mr. Brockey, chairman of the United Appeal board of trustees, was talking about that translation.

"Churches and schools prepare us to meet life wisely, he said. And gifts to United Appeal are 'a tangible expression of both.' "

Nowhere, observed Mr. Brockey, do people organize and shoulder the burden of voluntary charity on quite the scale seen in this country. They want to help, and the organized and systematic approach used in drives and campaigns—not as spontaneous and warmly personal, admittedly, as the old basket on the arm of a benevolent neighbor—is necessary because of the complexity of social and economic conditions. The alternative, said Mr. Brockey, would be to "surrender to complexity" and leave charity up to the government.

He didn't think Atlantans were about to surrender—and they weren't. The drive went over the top, dazzling everybody.

Personally, Mr. Brockey is widely believed to be a softhearted, sentimental kind of man, who adores and shamelessly spoils his own family and feels pangs of concern and compassion wherever he hears of pain and grief anywhere in the world but particularly in the world of Rich's. When Rich's people are ill or in trouble, he's said to be there—a flower sender, a note writer, an anxious telephone inquirer.

Needless to say, this is an image which Mr. Brockey himself does not care to have circulated.

"I'm tough," he says—and no employee would deny it. "I demand a lot of people. But then . . ." and his broad face softens in a smile . . . "I try to pick people who can and will do a lot."

Talking in the soft but even and rapid way which is the despair of stenographers and other notetakers, he goes on: "There's creativeness in merchandising. Excitement. In this business you must set goals but you can never be satisfied. You must reach a little farther, a little higher every time. There's no black magic in it. It's done by people."

In the Rich's tradition, Mr. Brockey is extremely active in many community enterprises, charitable, church, and civic, but he manages time for the wide and voracious reading which has been a habit of life. (With typical Brockey efficiency, to make time for all the books which attract him, he took a course in rapid reading. The result is that he often reads a book a night.) As an old furniture man, he is intensely interested in his home and has a part in all decisions on major redecorating or furniture-changing projects.

But then, say his associates, he is intensely interested in everything. The fashion experts say he is also an expert on clothes, with a highly developed sense of taste and an eye for quality.

Travel is a particular enthusiasm of his, and Rich's buyers in far corners of the world are never surprised to see their boss show up, inquiring into local production methods, assessing the quality of goods, and projecting the marketing possibilities at home.

Vice President and Mrs. Joseph F. Asher have traveled abroad many times with Mr. and Mrs. Brockey, making an extended trip around the world in 1966. Both Brockeys are easy and delightful traveling companions, says Mr. Asher, but Mr. Brockey sometimes awes him.

"He wants to see everything everywhere," according to Mr.

Asher. "I can only take so many cathedrals and museums per trip and sometimes I like to go back to the hotel and take a nap. Harold Brockey—never."

If this be restlessness, Mr. Brockey is inclined to make the most of it. Indeed, he has been known to advocate restlessness for department stores. It engenders a healthy questioning: "What else could we have done?" "How could we have done it better?"

Louis Carrol, Senior Vice President in Charge of Merchandising and Publicity, who first came to Rich's from Bamberger's in New Jersey, has watched his chief operate for years and he never ceases to marvel at the way he picks people and warms and encourages them and pushes them toward their best development.

Some executives make the mistake of picking good people and either abandoning them or "smothering and dominating" them, Mr. Carrol points out. President Brockey keeps his hands on the reins but he drives with a light rein, giving support and direction when they are needed, he says.

Mr. Carrol's broad experience enabled him to succeed Mr. Brockey as General Merchandise Manager of the Store for Homes in 1955. He advanced rapidly from that post to Senior Vice President in Charge of Merchandising and Publicity for the total organization.

As a young man, Mr. Carrol planned to be a lawyer and was a student at New Jersey Law School "because I love logic." He gave up law for retailing when he decided to get married and did not want to put his family through the exigencies of stinting so he could do graduate work at one of the bigger universities.

But he never lost his enthusiasm for logic and the "clarity and decisiveness" with which Harold Brockey directs Rich's operation appeal to him greatly. In addition, he revels in the catholicity of Mr. Brockey's far-roaming, voracious intelligence.

"He's interested in as many things as there are in the

world," Mr. Carrol says of his boss. "He reads with enormous breadth and latitude. Besides that," he sums up with a sudden infectious grin, "he's a very, very keen merchant."

Mr. Carrol is himself a keen merchant to whom all Rich's merchandising staff reports.

As Senior Vice President and General Merchandise Manager, Mr. Carrol considers he has the stimulating job of "working with the experts, the pros," that is, the other vice presidents in charge of the myriad goods and services the store offers. As liaison man, he sees ideas and projects when they are aborning, and on him rests the ultimate responsibility of "making sure what we want to happen does happen" in acquiring and presenting the right image with the type of service and merchandise Rich's is famous for.

"Working with experts is no problem," says Mr. Carrol, but there is one place where he admits to being super careful, and that is to not discourage creativity which would thwart people with talent. The better method, he says, is to "stretch people beyond their capabilities with training and guidance— give them horizons to shoot for and make sure the standard of performance is maintained."

Kenneth P. Mages is both financial vice president and treasurer. A native of Milwaukee and graduate of Marquette University, he was a partner in the nationally known auditing firm of Touche, Ross, Bailey & Smart when Rich's persuaded him to come to Atlanta. Rich's had long been a client of his firm and he had handled enough department store accounts to be familiar with the work, which was fortunate because he entered the store to find it in the throes of its first computer pains.

Computers had been installed and were smartly whipping out monthly statements to Rich's customers, but the early bugs in the system were numerous and the howls of outrage from customers were loud and vociferous. They did not understand new "coded" bills, where you had to look up numbers and letters to find out what you were being charged for instead of the old-time cozy description, "Cotton gloves, $1.98." Hundreds of them thought they had been wrongly charged and everybody was muttering mutinously.

Looking back, Mr. Mages thinks the new computer system wouldn't have been such a headache if it had been introduced in a more leisurely fashion. When the bugs were worked out and the feathers of irate customers smoothed, the computer went on with the billing in a style that had the double advantage of being lightning fast and acceptable to the public.

By 1966 two big computers valued at more than a million dollars were running twenty hours a day, sometimes seven days a week, handling a multitude of fiscal matters that in Morris Rich's day were handled by ink-stained gentlemen in sleeve holders and eyeshades. It is, Mr. Mages predicts, only the beginning. He foresees the time when the computer center, which is under his general supervision and the direct supervision of Ed Lange, will take the drudgery out of inventory control, for instance. Harassed buyers will no longer have to put in long hours checking their stock but the computers will keep a running account of sales, storing up knowledge on the history of past sales, to give a buyer instant information on reordering. If a customer wants a brown sofa of a certain style the computers may soon advise the sales person the exact spot in the warehouse or suburban store where such a sofa is to be found.

There are eight vice presidents: Ben Tuck, vice president and general superintendent, who is responsible for seeing that Rich's tradition of customer service is adhered to; Joseph F. Asher, vice president and secretary, in charge of the Man's World, Boys Departments, and several other departments, including books; Peter Stelling, vice president in charge of the Store for Fashion; Joseph Watters, vice president in charge of the Store for Homes; Alvin Ferst, a vice president with a unique job of planning and maintenance, who reports directly to the president; Joel Goldberg, who heads the Budget Store;

John Miles, Sales Promotion; and Dudley Pope, Design & Display.

Joe Asher is the old-timer in this octet. His grandfather ran a livery business in Atlanta before the Civil War and his mother, the former Rebecca Davis, was born in 1863, even as the Battle of Atlanta was warming up. Mr. Asher started to work for Rich's as a shirt salesman on Whitehall Street in 1921 when shirts, long underwear, and high collars were his principal stock in trade. He was to marry a co-worker in 1933, the former Miss Helen Elsas, who worked at various times in the book, lamp, and china departments.

Mr. Asher launched one of the first career shops for men in the country and pioneered in establishing a department devoted exclusively to boys' clothing.

Despite, or maybe because of, his long service in the arena of masculine fashions, Mr. Asher was amiably unperturbed when the revolution in clothes for teen-age youth boiled up in England a year or so ago. Although one to counsel conservatism in haberdashery generally, Mr. Asher, like the other leaders at Rich's, is mindful of the whims and caprices of youth. He found what some people were calling the "weird" getups of young "mods" in England at the very least interesting and, to some extent, a "wonderful stimulant" to the teen-age group. He predicted that with some modification and liberal applications of good taste what seemed weird might win a place for itself in America and the South. To get ready for it he prepared for the establishment of a "gear shop," which would offer Atlanta youth the best of the new look.

Peter Stelling reflects the same attitude in dealing with the "kooky" fashions for young females. The bold, the amusing, and the offbeat are to be found in girls' gear shops to keep the young happy and "in," even as their elders shop for the muted classics.

Mr. Stelling, a Floridian, got into fashion following his graduation as a music major from Rollins College because depression was on the land and the country wasn't ready for another Rudy Vallee. He did sing some over the radio, auditioned in New York for Paul Whiteman, and performed for experimental television in 1932. The Columbia Broadcasting System had a few sets and was trying the thing out and young Mr. Stelling, movie star handsome and six feet two, had a go at it. The camera was fixed and so, perforce, was the performer. He had to stand in footprints painted on the floor and keep his head in a picture frame hung from the ceiling at a height comfortable for a man five feet two.

Prophetically, one of the songs he gave his limited television audience was "Georgia on My Mind." It wasn't, then. He went home to Orlanda and went to work in the local "nice" store, Yowell-Drew, selling men's clothing, to await his big break in music. When they offered to raise him from eighteen to thirty-five dollars a week to take on women's fashions, he was so dazzled by the opportunities in retailing he forgot about music, except to head up such enterprises as the Atlanta Symphony and the Municipal Theatre nowadays.

The newest vice president, Joel Goldberg, a native of Worcester, Massachusetts, and a graduate of Dartmouth College, had served a seven-year apprenticeship in retailing with the Boston store, Filene's, when he came to Rich's to work as a buyer in the fashion department.

Joel Goldberg moved into what used to be known as the bargain basement for the express purpose of upgrading it. Now called the Budget Store, this division aims to offer quality merchandise at the lowest possible price, in line with the Rich's policy of providing all things to all kinds of customers.

It is Mr. Goldberg's theory that his division appeals not only to low-income people but to the same kind of customer who might buy a Specialty Shop dress on occasion and a piece of Steuben glass now and then. Everybody has to be thrifty somewhere, he theorizes, but that does not mean that they are willing to forego quality and make do with shoddy goods or poor workmanship.

By assiduous searching, careful buying, and a sound style sense, Mr. Goldberg and his buyers cope manfully with the old cliché that you get what you pay for—striving to hold the price low and keep the quality up.

As director of promotion, Vice President John Miles heads one of the busiest and most often honored advertising departments in the country. Rich's buys reams of space in all kinds of publications but particularly in the daily newspapers, in addition to radio, television, and a limited amount of billboard advertising. The store's color ads regularly bring home top awards from national contests, and once in a regional contest Mr. Miles and his fifty-three copywriters and artists copped twelve out of twenty-two possible prizes.

In 1964 the National Retail Merchants Association awarded Rich's gold medal for its "most notable Christmas campaign . . . which was characterized by the judges as one of great brilliance in its use of color advertising and exciting layout design."

The store recently won *Editor & Publisher's* award for "continuous, consistent creative use of color in retail advertising" and the Newspaper Advertising Executive Association selected Rich's as one of the fifteen best color advertisers in the country.

Of course, the institutional ads, inaugurated by Frank Neely, have long been famous and regularly harvest prizes. One to make the textbooks and to be reprinted often shows a measles-spattered moppet mourning, "I wish I had got my measles at Rich's so I could return 'em."

John Miles thinks institutional advertising is one of the most effective ways of reaching the public, but he happens to believe wholeheartedly in all kinds of advertising—"and plenty of it."

John Miles came to Rich's from W. & J. Sloane in 1959. He is a native of Illinois, was graduated from the University of Illinois and did graduate work at Northwestern, majoring in art and advertising. He is the father of three sons.

The future is ever-present in the minds of all Rich's executives. Atlanta, a burgeoning city, is always bursting out at the seams, competition is fast and aggressive, and planning is a constant, swift-moving current that catches up everybody a part of every day.

Nowhere does it reach flood tide more often than in the office of Vice President Alvin Ferst on the sixth floor of the Store for Homes. Mr. Ferst came to Rich's via Georgia Tech, where he majored in industrial engineering, Philco, and a wartime spell with the Seabees in Trinidad, where he helped to build, maintain, and tear down a base several times before vacating it.

Like many another Georgia Tech graduate, when he decided to come home to Georgia after the war, he sought out that famed old grad, Frank Neely, for advice and counsel on the job hunt. He hadn't thought of applying to Mr. Neely and Rich's for a job. In fact, he didn't think the retail business would interest him much but before the interview was over Mr. Neely, with characteristic bluntness, said, "Aw, hell, let's go to work!"

It took a while but eventually Alvin Ferst did come back to Rich's where he was soon plunged into converting space in the big Candler warehouse into a fast-moving, smooth-functioning receiving station for Rich's goods. It was a rush job of such dimensions that Mr. Ferst and Bruce Smith, who was then chief of industrial engineering, spread out an eight-foot swatch of tracing paper, conferred, and started drawing toward each other from the ends, meeting in the middle. When they had completed the plan, Mr. Ferst, the old Seabee, was dispatched to supervise the installation in the warehouse. That was a day-and-night job for a matter of weeks and when it was finished he launched a research planning project for the Store for Homes. Today Alvin Ferst's department, staffed by eight industrial engineers, four time study specialists, and

assorted architects and builders, is ever in the midst of building or investigating, analyzing, and making recommendations
about building.

The suburban store program has been their biggest challenge in recent years. An experiment in what Mr. Rich calls
an "outpost" was a small store in the Belvedere Shopping
Center, which opened south of Decatur in adjoining DeKalb
County. It made no pretense of being a complete store and it
was such a success that before the foundations had settled
good, Mr. Ferst and his staff were planning to expand it skyward.

Lenox Square in northeast Atlanta was the second venture
into the suburbs—a complete department store, which started
with three floors, totaling 180,000 square feet, and has not
stopped growing since. It opened in 1959. As successful as
this venture is out on Peachtree Road it did not strike Rich's
management as really ideal to go into a spot which somebody
else had developed. They liked the idea of being in on the
developing, and promptly got to work with all the complicated
economic sleuthing it takes to pick a shopping center.

The result was three new shopping centers, Rich's-initiated
—one in Cobb County west of the Lockheed plant, one in
north DeKalb County, and one in west Fulton County known
as the Greenbriar Shopping Center. In these instances Rich's
acquired the land and planned the shopping center, picking
their own spot before opening it up to other merchants.

Mr. Ferst's staff, aided by the professional firm of business
analysts, Hammer, Greene, Siler Associates, went out on foot,
by automobile, and by helicopter to learn where the people
were, what their average income was, and what they might
be expected to want in the way of goods and services.
It was not, as Mr. Hammer put it, a feat of clairvoyance but
slow, slugging, painstaking searching for facts and figures.
They checked traffic patterns and studied the opportunities
for moving goods in and building storage and when they
were satisfied that Rich's would be needed in an area, they

acquired the land. The result was a two-story complete department store in Cobb County, a two-story complete department store on the enclosed, completely air-conditioned mall in DeKalb County, and a three-level building in Fulton County which reproduces on a smaller scale every department of the downtown store, all fraternally neighboring with dozens of smaller shops and stores joining the development.

A map of Atlanta which papers one wall of Mr. Ferst's office shows a little something about Rich's effort to keep its finger on the Atlanta pulse which is the envy of other businesses and many politicians. The five-county metropolitan area is divided into seven segments with its population growth indicated by colors—brown for 1959–61, for instance, green for 1961–62, yellow for 1962–63, red for 1963–64, and so on to the present. Masses of black pins indicate apartment dwellers, one pin for every ten units.

Naturally Rich's existing stores are clearly defined on this map, but less clearly defined are two quiet little circles designating two tracts of land, seventy-five to one hundred acres each, which Rich's has bought for the future. Within five years these will be developed, if all the signs and omens auger well, and in the meantime the experts are looking at five other large cities in Georgia with even more branches in mind.

In addition to the executives in the store Rich's has on its board of directors the talents of many outstanding business leaders of the area. Among these are: Howard Dobbs, Jr., president of the Life Insurance Company of Georgia; Ben S. Gilmer, executive vice president, American Telephone & Telegraph Company; Joseph K. Heyman, senior vice president of the Trust Company of Georgia; A. Carl Kotchian, executive vice president of Lockheed Aircraft; Walter M. Mitchell, vice president of the Draper Corporation; Louis Montag, senior partner of Montag and Caldwell; Oscar R. Strauss, Jr., of Selig Manufacturing Company; and Robert B. Troutman, Sr., the eminent Atlanta attorney.

9

WOMEN AT WORK

"Have engaged Madame Marie Gillette, formerly of Paris, France. . . . Let the Ladies Know This."

This message, profligately telegraphed home by Morris to Emanuel in 1881, presaged a new day in the operation of the store.

Morris was in New York searching for a "name" modiste to head the important Dressmaking Department. This was the only department where it had been deemed suitable for women to work. Ready-to-wear was an untrustworthy infant then. But four years later, perhaps under the influence of the charming Madame Gillette, the store announced "a new departure—young ladies at the kid glove counter who will fit the glove to your hand. (These gloves are warranted not to break.)"

By a quaint paradox women workers had, through the glove department, got their foot in the door. From that day on, they were *in*.

Today Rich's is one of the region's premier employers of women. In 1967 an estimated six thousand women work at Rich's, full-time and part-time, constituting about two-thirds of all employees.

Morris Rich, the father of daughters, might be pleased to see the delicate impress of the feminine hand on his business.

In January 1961 Rich's took a black-bordered ad in the

Constitution to mourn the death of one of its more famous female executives, Miss Annie Mae Gallagher.

Miss Annie Mae, daughter of an Irish policeman, went to work for Morris at the age of fourteen years as a package wrapper and became a still-revered voice in fashion in the South.

She was the forerunner of the legions of buyers for all departments who now travel the world looking for clothes, jewelry, silver, china, linens, furniture, and other household pretties for the women of the South. She trained another young Irish girl, Catherine Rice, who started in the Whitehall Street store, also at the age of fourteen, and became one of the first women merchandise managers, progressing to a position on the store's board of directors. Miss Rice retired a few years ago with a record of fifty years' service at Rich's, leaving behind many chic, knowledgeable young women, in whom she inculcated both the rudiments of smart buying and smart merchandising and a large and tender regard for Rich's.

Among these is Marianne Lambert, whose uncle, James P. Flynn, started at Rich's as a wrapper in 1897 and was a director at the time of his death in 1948. Mr. Flynn was credited with making Rich's yard goods department, particularly the silk section, outstanding in the region. He became buyer for the silk and dress goods department in 1914 when it had three sales people. Within a decade the department had thirty sales people and the colorful, Irish Mr. Flynn was widely sought as an authority on fabrics.

But "Uncle Jimmy" did not think his niece, Marianne, should work at Rich's, and when she finished Visitation Convent in Georgetown in 1934 she applied for a summer job without his knowledge. Her first assignment was addressing envelopes for a direct mail campaign—a job she handled with such neatness and dispatch that she caught the eye of Miss Rice and was hired full-time.

As a full-time employee she was entrusted with the responsible job of taking each day's invoices to David H. Strauss, a vice president in charge of finance, so he could check them over and make sure the buyers had received cash discounts. (Today the volume of invoices is so great it is beyond any one man's attention and is handled by the individual buyers themselves.)

Young Miss Lambert's next assignment was one which she was, by upbringing and early interest, well equipped to take on—the selling of silver. Rich's stocked only new silver then and its entire silver stock was contained in two or three cases in a center aisle on the main floor. Marianne's mother had long been fond of antique silver and the girl had studied patterns and hallmarks as a hobby. As soon as she was assigned to sell silver she took up a serious study of it and right after World War II, in 1946, two of the first American buyers to hit the old silver markets of England and Ireland were Miss Catherine Rice and her protégée, Marianne Lambert.

It happened that it was a cold winter day and Marianne wore some wool-lined leather gloves as she handled the old serving pieces from ancient castles. The ones she picked out to buy for sale in Georgia were such a phenomenal success that Rich's stayed in the antique silver business—and Marianne Lambert has never been to market since without her wool-lined leather gloves.

Her friends call these now considerably worn gloves "Marianne's silver pickers" and insist that one of the first things she does when she returns from a buying trip to Europe is to have her gloves cleaned and stored in a vault.

Miss Lambert, a devout Roman Catholic, laughingly denies such superstitious care of the gloves—but she does admit that she never goes to market without them.

Marianne Lambert is one of two women to hold the executive post of division merchandise manager. The other one is Mrs. Elizabeth Runyan, a young widow, who specializes in junior fashions, lingerie, foundations, and sleepwear. In addition to her special field of antique silver, Miss Lambert supervises a number of buyers, most of them women and recognized names in their respective fields. Mrs. Gertrude Church, in handbags and gloves, came to Rich's in 1931, when Chamberlin, Johnson & DuBose Company became a victim of the depression and closed its doors. Mrs. Dovie Johnson has been the hosiery buyer for more than thirty years. There's Vivian Millican in costume jewelry, Marian Finley, cosmetics, and Valeria Cooper, who buys the silver which doesn't fall into the antique category.

In the early days the more elegant home furnishings were the special interest of the younger Rich brother, Emanuel. He went to market and brought back so many things Rich's had to take additional space—20 and 22 Hunter Street—in 1890 to house its carpet and drapery department. That same year M. Rich & Bros. won eight medals and twenty-five dollars cash at the Piedmont Exposition for its house furnishings and accessories.

The list of prizewinners included:
1. Best display of Oriental and decorated chinaware. 2. Best display of Bisque and Parian ware. 3. Fancy lamps, trimmings, etc. 4. Carpets (medal and an additional twenty-five dollars). 5. Rugs. 6. Draperies. 7. Statuary. 8. Lions and busts.

Today two of the departments which undoubtedly would draw Emanuel's intense interest are run by women—china, and gifts which Mrs. Frances Hughes assembles from all over the world; and the Connoisseur Gallery, managed by Mrs. William Campbell, wife of a well-known author. Mrs. Campbell, the former Miss Lila Cothran of New Orleans, was reared among beautiful old furniture and for a time had her own shop in Rome, Georgia. She went to work in Rich's as a saleswoman and took the job of running its antique shop on trial six years ago. It has been a happy association for both.

The snobbish notion that only the rich, the well-born, and the cultivated deserve the old and the beautiful is one Mrs.

Campbell has devoted some time to dispelling. The layaway plan works as well among Queen Anne tea tables and ancient Spanish armoires as anywhere. In fact, Mrs. Campbell delights in seeing a beauty operator with a yen for a seven-hundred-dollar Meissen jar "pay down on it," and she cheers when a young girl in blue jeans persuades her family to forgo an expensive wedding for her and give her the $295 English bowfront chest of 1780 vintage to grace her new living room.

Exchange and return are also well known in this department. She once took back a twenty-five-hundred-dollar Adam breakfront from a man who had it six or eight months—and was glad to do it because a little extra age on a piece so venerable does no harm. But despite the liberal store policy on these matters Mrs. Campbell thought it was too much when a woman sent back some chairs, reproductions, that she had been using for six years.

"I gave her a bit of a fight," grinned the small, dark-eyed buyer, "but she knew she had me. The best I could salvage was 20 per cent, which she thought was 'fair' for using them six years!"

Twice a year a U. S. Customs inspector from Baltimore comes to the old Candler warehouse in southwest Atlanta for the express purpose of admitting to this country Rich's shipments of antiques from abroad. He is an expert in his field, so attuned to antiquity that he can almost tell at a glance the true age of a piece of furniture. If it was made prior to 1830 it is admitted duty free.

So for these periods Atlanta, an inland city, is known to the U. S. Government as the "Port of Atlanta." It is a title which would make Morris and Emanuel very proud.

The care and feeding of celebrities was not a problem with the early Rich's. Show people sought out the store in the days when Lucian W. York was its manager, from 1911 to 1924, because Mr. York had a particular affinity for them. He had been an autograph collector from boyhood, when he took up tickets at one of the Atlanta theaters, and he continued to be a dedicated patron of the theater. For years many minstrel companies and road show troupes that came to town made a point of marching down Whitehall Street to look up Mr. York and sometimes to serenade him.

Far from marching sturdily into the store and spontaneously making with the music, modern celebrities are frequently unbelievably cosseted. These days those who come to Rich's fall generally into two classifications—Authors and Assorted.

Both classifications of celebrity, it happens, fall under the purview of women executives, the book buyer, Faith Brunson, and the public relations director, Anne Poland.

Faith is an alumnus of public relations where, fresh out of college in her native Mississippi, she started as a secretary in 1945 "to see what working in the city was like." Her experience with celebrities has ranged from hair-raising to hilarious. She has seen alcoholic authors disappear five minutes before they were to sit down and take pen in hand for a multitude of adoring fans. She has put hats on clerks and marched them by to pretend they were readers when a sterling but unread author, who had asked invitations for three thousand people, was left sitting all alone with his prose. She has comforted fearful lady murder mystery writers and curbed the blackmailing instincts of delicate vanity published poets seeking eye-for-an-eye vengeance on people obligated to them socially, financially, or politically. And once, when the Atlanta *Journal's* dog editor, John Woodward, was autographing a volume called, *Butch, Diary of a Dog,* she made welcome dozens of yapping dogs and yowling cats his fans brought to the party to do him homage.

Miss Brunson happened to still be in public relations when her predecessor as book buyer, Mrs. Georgia Leckie, lost a famous novelist minutes before he was to make a speech and autograph books. The gentleman was a celebrated *bon vivant* and it seemed elementary to everybody that he was off somewhere tippling. Roswell Smith, the store protection chieftain, marshaled his men and sent them off to check the local pubs.

In the midst of the search Mrs. Leckie suddenly remembered that the author, a soft-hearted ex-newspaperman, had a penchant for buying bicycles for orphans when he drank. She hastily checked the bicycle department and found that three bicycles had just been dispatched to a local children's home.

Detective Smith and Mrs. Leckie rushed to the scene where the novelist, mellow with drink but by no means incapacitated, was giving bicycle riding lessons to a group of ecstatic moppets.

Actress Gloria Swanson, in town to promote a line of dresses in which she was interested, is one celebrity Faith still remembers with awe bordering on incredulity.

It was not too long after Miss Swanson's comeback in the movie, *Sunset Boulevard,* that Faith met her at the railroad station and conveyed her to the Biltmore Hotel. She did not know then that Miss Swanson was a woman of many whims and crotchets and she was totally unprepared for what happened when the actress walked into the hotel elevator. First, the operator, an old Swanson fan, was so undone by the privilege of transporting her idol skyward that she was totally immobilized. She made no effort to start her vehicle but stood there drinking in the vision of the famous retroussé nose, the tip-tilted blue eyes, and the still-raven locks until Miss Swanson spun around and announced that she was walking.

"She not only had claustrophobia, I found out later," explained Miss Brunson, "but she was a physical fitness buff. She climbed all the way to her suite on the ninth floor. I took out after her and after about three days of climbing and several draughts of oxygen from a pulmotor squad I caught up with her. She was busy flinging open all the windows, letting in a lot of *freezing* fresh air!"

Before Faith could catch her breath the actress had taken a

quick inventory of the room and asked crisply, "Where are the flowers?"

"The flowers?" mumbled Faith. "Oh, er, I'll see . . ."

The young public relations director had just that week launched an economy campaign for her department and had ruled flowers for visiting celebrities as an unnecessary frill. From the look in Miss Swanson's eye she realized her error.

"I went back downstairs as fast as I could—*by elevator*—and ordered everything they had in the flower shop, stuck Mr. Dick's card in it, and sent it right up. Her room looked exactly like one of Patterson's finest funerals . . ."

And with all those windows open to the winter air it was about the right temperature for keeping both flowers and a body, as Faith remembers it.

The rest of Miss Swanson's visit was punctuated with surprises. In her honor Mr. Rich gave a small, select luncheon, to which the actress brought her own banana and a vocal disdain for the shrimp cocktail and rare roast beef the other guests were enjoying. When Miss Swanson called time out from narrating a fashion show of her dress line Faith led her to the store clinic, thinking she might want to lie down a moment. Instead, the nimble Miss Swanson flopped to the floor, flung her small body into the air, and spent her rest period standing on her head.

Her fans turned out to be legion—old-timers who remembered her from the days of silent movies and youngsters who had just met her in *Sunset Boulevard*. And they packed Rich's for a glimpse of her. At the end of the day Miss Swanson just had time to make her train and Faith arranged to get her through the store and out to a waiting limousine as quickly as possible. This bypassed hordes of fans, but one persistent lady caught up with the actress as she reached her car.

Fixing her with an adoring look, she cried, "This is the most *wonderful* day of my life!"

"Well, it shouldn't be!" snapped the actress, leaping into the car and slamming the door.

Except for that unfortunate last-minute lapse in public relations, Miss Brunson is inclined to agree with the fan. If it wasn't a *"wonderful"* day, at least it had its moments.

Writers are probably the least colorful of the celebrities who come to Rich's, but when an author is also an actor, things start humming. Bob Hope, in town to autograph *I Owe Russia $1200*, was a complete delight to his fans and his hosts. Anne Poland found out somewhere that he and Mrs. Hope collect Steuben glass, and the store was able to find in its extensive Steuben stock a small duck that by happy coincidence had a nose just like the comic's. This was presented to Mr. Hope.

Bob was so captivated with the gift that for several weeks in his travels about the country he charmingly displayed it to newspaper and television interviewers.

"We got a lot of mileage out of that duck," Miss Poland has remarked with pardonable satisfaction. "I remember one UPI story . . ."

When actress Billie Burke, the old Ziegfeld follies beauty and widow of the famed impresario, Flo Ziegfeld, wrote a book, *A Feather on My Nose*, Rich's invited her to come to lunch and to autograph her opus.

In town for one day, Miss Burke arrived with nine pieces of luggage, including three fur coats and several dozen photographs of her late husband, all of which she unpacked. Miss Brunson went out to her hotel to take her to the luncheon and had to telephone back to the store and tell them to return the fruit cup to the cooler—Miss Burke was cutting and washing her hair and looking for her freckle cream!

When she did get to the store, casually flopping against her ankles as she walked a drawstring brown cloth bag containing one hundred thousand dollars in jewels, the fluttery Miss Burke was completely winsome, delighting store executives and book customers alike.

Miss Nancy Hopkins, daughter of a pioneer Atlanta jurist, Judge John Livingston Hopkins, is the dean of Rich's booksellers, starting there more than thirty years ago. She has directed the reading habits and molded the tastes of three generations of young Georgians, an endeavor she considers so holy a cause that many Atlanta parents have but one criterion for selecting books for their children: "Does Miss Nancy recommend it?" She will go to infinite trouble to get hard-to-find classics and out-of-print books she feels are needed by some young reader. And although she is a gentlewoman of the most southern school, she can be very firm with parents who underestimate a child's need of books. On one occasion she heard a mother quibbling over buying her daughter a book of Emily Dickinson poems, which the child ached to own, because she had just finished buying her curtains and a bedspread for her room.

"My dear," said Miss Hopkins, "it's lovely to have furnished her room but aren't you fortunate that she wants to furnish her mind?"

The mother looked surprised and then thoughtful and then she agreed. The child got the poems—and, as time went on, many more mind-furnishing books.

For all her solemn dedication to the cause of books for children, Miss Hopkins takes a hoydenish pleasure in the lighter moments of bookselling and the wildly varied challenge it presents.

"How do you plant sweet peas, how many eggs in an egg custard, have you got an Old Testament with how to save souls on the edges and is this rhythm method any good?"

Miss Nancy rattles off a sampling of a day's questions AND the answers:

"Six or eight inches deep in the fall and mulch . . . four

eggs to a quart of milk . . . alphabet on the edges, the rest is inside . . . I wouldn't trust it, if I were you, but we do have a book that might help you."

Miss Nancy has seen many celebrities come and go. Her lifelong friend, Margaret Mitchell, had but one autographing party—this at Davison's where Mrs. Luise Sims, another long-time friend of the author, was then the book buyer. But she came to Rich's and autographed until the book turned out to be such a runaway success her publishers recommended that she autograph no more. To this day Rich's gets orders for copies of *Gone with the Wind*, with the specification that it be "autographed please."

She remembers many authors with affection: Thomas Wolfe ("He was lovely. I just stood there and gazed at him. Sweet as a rose.") Marjorie Kinnan Rawlings, Richard Halliburton, the shy young Georgia mountain poet, Byron Herbert Reece, and countless others. But the most memorable of autograph parties was one the store gave for a then local writer, young Harry Lee, on the publication of his first book, *Fox in the Cloak*, in 1938.

Just before time for the party to start the skies opened up with a record-breaking deluge, which flooded the streets and then settled down to a heavy, steady rain.

"Not a soul came," Miss Hopkins recalls. "But that precious Harry was as good as gold about it. He was awed that the day his book was published should be so calamitous. First the cloudburst—and then Hitler marched into Czechoslovakia!"

People who are resoundingly successful in other fields often are irresistibly drawn to bookselling for some mysterious reason. This is true of most of Rich's clerks. Mrs. George Goldstein, a former English teacher, is one and so is Mrs. Mary Lou Dority, both of whom have been at Rich's more than fifteen years, adroitly fielding strange questions and coping with requests that often are half misinformation, half malapropism. Without a moment's hesitation they can find Emily Brontë's "*Withering*" *Heights* or that "great children's classic, A. A. Milne's *Minnie, the Moocher*—and tactfully look the other way while the customer discovers it is *Wuthering Heights* and *Winnie-the-Pooh*.

Rich's is by all odds the biggest bookseller in the area and the scene of innumerable autograph parties. Its critics point out that the store will send out invitations and trot out the tea and cookies even for authors who pay to have their works published. Miss Brunson good-humoredly admits it.

"If we can work it out we love to have parties for all Georgia authors," she says. "And no matter what the book is, if it was written by a Georgian we stock at least five copies of it."

The assumption being that *everybody* has that many friends.

Sometimes it is not books but related stock, such as the "brush stroke" reproductions of great pictures, that present the greatest challenge to Miss Brunson's department. The staff remembers happily the lady who asked if Van Gogh's famous "Sunflowers" came in any other color. Then there was the customer who wanted Salzman's "Head of Christ" but was disappointed when she saw it because it came in tones of brown.

"I always thought of Jesus' eyes as being blue," the customer said wistfully. "I wonder if Rich's could . . . ?"

"Certainly," said Miss Brunson staunchly. And she whisked the picture to the store's art director, Fred Bohrman, who deftly painted over the brown eyes with cerulean blue.

"It was a knockout," Miss Brunson recalls. "The customer was so pleased she wanted to pay extra for it but I told her I was just glad our art director had that opportunity. I felt like it had made his day."

Of course public relations takes an interest in all celebrities, Authors or Assorted, and Anne Poland, a slim, sunny-dispositioned young Alabamian, who also got her start as a secretary, combines the grace and good sense necessary to ride herd on the tempestuous and the temperamental.

An aging spoiled actress, who had agreed to be the guest of honor at one large party in town while she was at Rich's modeling clothes, decided at the last minute that she wouldn't go. It was a cocktail party and she used that as an excuse.

"I don't HAVE to go," she said petulantly, still lounging in her bed when Miss Poland went by her hotel to pick her up. "I don't even drink."

Miss Poland equably pointed out that the hosts would be disappointed but agreed that the actress did not HAVE to go. She left quietly without even asking why a non-drinker had so many empty beer bottles beside her bed.

Fortunately, most celebrities are pure pleasure to their hosts and Miss Poland remembers with gratitude people like the famed cosmetician, Elizabeth Arden, who, at Rich's request, sponsored with money and her presence a "Christmas Trees Around the World" exhibit, which the local Cherokee Garden Club puts on annually at the Atlanta Art Association. Helena Rubenstein, also in cosmetics, was another happy guest. There have been scores of fashion greats, designers, and even such distinguished wearers of clothes as the late Adolphe Menjou, who helped officiate at the opening of the new and expanded Store for Men in 1951.

The volume celebrities, of course, are the ones indigenous to the region and these are the special concern of another feminine employee, Kitty (Mrs. James) Lofton, also in public relations.

One Christmas season several years ago the mayor of Chattanooga looked out on his town's main street and saw nine Greyhound buses lined up to take the women of Chattanooga to Rich's in Atlanta to do their shopping.

It was enough to give a politician apoplexy. Hoping to remedy the situation before the merchants of Chattanooga noticed the buses, the mayor got on the radio and appealed to the better natures of the Rich's-bound ladies to stay home and shop.

It was too late.

One of their number, a zealous garden clubber, had heard of Rich's plan whereby women's clubs all over Georgia and Alabama could have spend-the-day parties in the store. Buses and sometimes trains and planes are chartered and for a flat fee a woman can pay her round-trip fare and a little something extra into her club's treasury. Rich's makes a contribution to the treasury, too, pins a "VIP" (for Very Important Person) ribbon on each lady, and treats her to lunch and to tea, usually with music and flowers and some slight gift as a memento of her visit.

It was, the lady felt, more than the Tennessee Federation of Garden Clubs should be called upon to give up, especially at the last minute. So she and her colleagues turned resolute backs on the mayor's appeal and headed south. Spend-the-day groups still come from Chattanooga and all parts of Tennessee, although not in nine-busload lots any more. Mrs. Lofton regrets this but philosophically accepts it as probably just as well because "Mr. Dick wouldn't like it if we got the Chattanooga merchants mad at us."

Any year's total of VIP's runs around twenty thousand, and red-haired Kitty Lofton greets each new wave with genuine enthusiasm. As they arrive she goes out to meet them, pinning their VIP ribbons on them, giving them a store directory and a shopping bag and asking solicitously, "Do you need a charge account?" If they do, they get it on the spot—a practice which would cause an ordinary credit manager's hair to turn white overnight. Rich's George L. Griffeth thinks it's great.

"These ladies are top-flight citizens," he says. "No risk involved in offering them credit."

Oddly enough, his records bear this out.

Lunch for the visitors is always a box lunch, which they can eat when they find a convenient pause in their shopping.

But toward the late afternoon when the VIPs' energy is flagging and their shopping bags are bulging, they meet on the sixth floor in the Magnolia Room, where candles on the tea table burn softly, Frances Wallace plays restorative show tunes on the organ, and Mrs. Lofton takes the microphone to recognize them, club by club, and to hand around handsomely gift-wrapped door prizes.

It is folksy and warm and just as personal as it was back in Morris Rich's little store of the 1880's, when they took an ad in the paper to let some customer know she had dropped her gold watch in Rich's and they were holding it for her.

10

FUN AND FESTIVITY

Two newcomers to Rich's public relations staff witnessed what they thought was an odd manifestation of spring toward the end of April last year. They both began having trouble with the telephone. When they answered often there would be no sound at all from the other end of the line—and sometimes there would be the sound of breathing, excited, slightly asthmatic breathing.

"Don't hang up, speak louder," directed older hands in the office. "It's somebody calling about the birthday party."

And, of course, it was, for from the middle of April to the first week in May everybody in the Southeast who is eighty years old or older begins to call in to firm up plans for their and Rich's annual birthday party. Rich's gives the party but the guests do not take lightly the responsibility of making it, as they say, sparkle.

Mr. Parks Hosey, who was ninety in 1966, calls in to discuss the songs he will sing. His rendition of "When I Grow Too Old to Dream" broke 'em up last year. What about something peppier like "God Bless America"? Mr. Roy Hartwell, in his eighties, and for years a wheelhorse in the Oak Hill Presbyterian Church choir, is considering starting with "How Great Thou Art" and winding up with "May God Bless You and Keep You." Miss Layona Glenn, the retired missionary who celebrated her one hundredth birthday by taking a trip around the world and going to call on President Johnson, will be back in time for the party and it's possible she will give her famous demonstration of touching the floor with her fingertips.

There's the eighty-year-old lady who has been going to Fred Astaire and may do a spot of dancing, and the poet from High View, the old folks' home, who will do humorous readings. Her perennial hit is entitled, "I Ain't Dead Yet."

These plans engross the guests for weeks ahead and take considerable talking over with the girls in Rich's public relations department. There's also the annual wistful call from an old lady who hopes to cop "The Oldest" prize every year. She has been nosed out for years by an indomitable old girl a few months her senior. Every April she calls up to chat about the party and to ask casually, "How is Mrs. ———? Have you heard from her yet?" There's a long silence at the other end of the line when the girls report that they have heard and she is in health.

And there are, of course, always a few who want the iron-clad age requirement bent a little in their direction.

"Do you really have to be eighty to come?" one lady asked.

"Yes, ma'am, eighty's the age requirement."

"Well, I'm seventy-seven—an *old* seventy-seven," the caller offered hopefully.

Public relations is regretful but adamant. The party was launched in 1947 on Rich's eightieth birthday as the eighty-year party and that's what it continues to be—for those eighty years old or older and, of course, the inevitable few who will fib about their age.

The afternoon in early May when the party is held sees every employee in Rich's who can get there on the sixth floor in front of the tea room, volunteering to pin carnations on the guests of honor or to help seat them. Of all the parties the store has this is the one closest to its heart.

The Magnolia Room is decorated to the hilt with bunting, balloons, and Confederate flags. Organist Frances Wallace

and accordionist Ward Duvall alternate with lively music.
Dwight Horton, director of employee activities, mans the
microphone to welcome the guests and to emcee the program
which will follow. There will be a fashion show, going back
to ante-bellum days and coming on up through the 1890's,
the 1920's, and the present. An old-time bathing suit revue
will bring appreciative whistles from some of the gentlemen.

There will be a gift of silver for the couple who have been
married the longest (sixty-eight years is about par), and one
for the guest with the most descendants. (Mrs. Florence
Green was a recent winner with 147.) The oldest man and
the oldest woman are singled out for gifts, as are the two who
came the greatest distance for the specific purpose of attending the party. (It doesn't count if you just happened to be
sojourning with your local descendants.) Those who have
lived in Atlanta the longest are saluted, given gifts and a
chance to reminisce. (Dr. George Bellinger, who was born
the year Rich's was, 1867, and knew the founder, Morris,
well, has been a famous raconteur and a frequent winner.)

When the candles on the birthday cakes are lighted, old
voices, some quavery and weak, some surprisingly strong, join
in singing "Happy Birthday." The playing of "Dixie" always
brings them to their feet cheering. (The first few birthday
parties the guests were treated to a genuine, spine-tingling
Rebel yell by the last of Georgia's Confederate veterans,
"General" William J. Bush, but since his death at the age of
104 there hasn't been an expert in that particular area.)

Dwight Horton always recites—and there are always those
who request copies of it—the well-known poem ending, "My
get-up-and-go has got up and went."

Among those who never miss the party if it can be helped
is Morris Rich's grandson, Dick. "Mr. Dick," as his employees
call him, circulates among the guests, visiting with them, and
if he makes a speech at all it is a brief and informal welcome.
He speaks of his grandfather, known to many of them, and
sometimes adds, "I wish he and my grandmother were here

today to see this magnificent assembly of strong people and fine people who helped to build this great city and who have been Rich's friends for all these years."

When the party is over and the old ladies in their flower-decked hats and the old gentlemen with their walking canes are led from the store by the one younger relative or friend invited to accompany each of them, the store nurses return to the clinic. The store doctor departs. And all the employees are a little misty-eyed that another birthday party has brought out so many of their favorite regulars.

Within a few days the thank-you notes come winging in, written in spidery, old-fashioned script and expressing graceful, old-fashioned appreciation.

"Dear Store," one woman wrote, "Yesterday was my first time to be invited to come to your famous eighty-year birth-day party." She went on to say that she had enjoyed it and ended: "We do not wonder that Atlanta's own Rich's is the store with the heart."

The birthday party, as dear as it is to hearts at Rich's, is but the high point in a year filled with parties, meetings, and festive goings and comings.

The Easter farm is an event planned for those at the other end of the age scale, little children, particularly those who have never had the privilege of patting a woolly baby lamb or exchanging gleeful "oinks" with a genuine, real live pig.

The production goes on a few weeks before Easter on the rooftop of the Store for Homes and attracts thousands of children.

As if making the acquaintance of chickens and ducks, lambs and pigs and rabbits were not exciting enough, Dudley Pope's display department brings out of mothballs the cele-brated Pink Pig, a skyborne railroad train on which the small fry ride. Formerly exclusively a Christmas attraction, The Pig may now reappear every Easter by popular demand. (So far there has been no effort to get the real live Santa Claus reindeer, another Christmas special, back for a midseason appearance. They continue to summer at a ranch at Stone Mountain.)

The Easter farm began in one of the Forsyth Street windows of the Store for Homes. In the daytime the window was open to children, who could pass through and talk with and pet the animals. At night passersby inspected it through the glass. That's how Mrs. Robert G. Watt happened to see a duckling in trouble one Sunday night. He was separated from his fellows and seemed to be caught in the wire of his pen.

Without a moment's hesitation Mrs. Watt did what practically any other Atlantan would have done—went to the nearest telephone and called Dick Rich at his home.

It was a little thing, she pointed out, but she knew Mr. Rich would thank her for calling and he did. The duckling was speedily rescued.

Probably all department stores worthy of the name celebrate the beginning of the fall season with a harvest sale and there's a mighty crush of bargain hunters and a cheerful symphony played on the cash register when Rich's has its. But the Harvest Sale at Rich's is launched by something peculiarly Richian in flavor and having more to do with fun and community interest than the cash register. It's the curb market.

For one day the length of the store on the block fronting Broad Street is turned into an open-air, country-style market where not Rich's but farm families from one end of the big agricultural state to the other bring their products to sell. There's a booth run by Alvin Todd, a mountain man who sells dahlia tubers. There's piccalilli and corn relish and sugarcane and sourwood honey, homegrown fryers and country-cured hams. The Home Demonstration Clubs of the state barbecue chickens over a sidewalk grill and 4-H Clubbers sell green vegetables, homebaked bread, and jewel-toned jars of jams and jellies.

For that one day it's not unusual to see dignified financiers and elegant social leaders moving about downtown proudly and nostalgically bearing stalks of sugarcane and damp sacks of turnip greens.

Perhaps remembering when cotton dropped disastrously and Georgia's economy with it, Rich's has always been particularly sympathetic with farm youth. Any project of the 4-H Clubs gets a hand at the store, and the dressmaking endeavors of eighteen young 4-H Club girls, who are selected to appear in the senior dress review at the annual state congress, get a special hand. These young women start by attending a fashion clinic at Rich's, where they see all the new fabrics and patterns and are given demonstrations in hairdo and makeup. Each girl receives from Rich's twenty-five dollars with which to buy the material for her dress, and when the last stitch is taken they all come back for lunch and a showing of their creations. The winner is announced that night at the climax of the State 4-H Club Congress.

Tours of the store are almost as numerous as tours of such on-purpose tourist attractions as the Cyclorama and Stone Mountain. Schoolchildren from throughout the state come and sight-see Rich's the way they do the state capitol, except if the store is expecting them there's always a Coke or ice cream party for them.

Every autumn Rich's gives a welcome party for all the new schoolteachers in Greater Atlanta. Those in the Atlanta city system are entertained at the downtown store, those in the DeKalb County system at Rich's North DeKalb, and those in the Decatur-DeKalb system at the new North DeKalb Shopping Center Rich's.

Kickoff luncheons and breakfasts for groups raising money for the heart fund, muscular dystrophy, and similar causes are frequently hosted by Rich's. High school home economists come for table-setting demonstrations by the store's experts, and Girl Scouts work out merit badges there.

The Auditorium in the Store for Homes is the regular meeting place of the Grandmothers Club, and once a year the grandmothers come for a special fashion show, replete with lunch and prizes for the youngest, the oldest, and the one with the most grandchildren.

It is also the place where the garden clubs of Georgia stage their four big flower shows each year. (The Garden Center, headquarters with a full-time director, is yet another thing Rich's furnishes these horticulturists.)

Any week's calendar for meet-and-eat gatherings in the store reveals a wide range of interest—mosquito control experts, the Needlework Guild, chiropractors, the Association of County Commissioners, Chaplains' Wives, the Georgia Hearing Aid Association, and regional waterworks officials.

The store even has its own advisory board of businesswomen, who meet once a month and have come up with suggestions which Rich's considers of invaluable aid in its effort to serve the working girl. Working girls, said this board, have to pay their bills on their lunch hour. Why not a box where they can drop off bill and payment without having to wait in line? Rich's adopted the suggestion.

They also asked why a one-hour-for-lunch woman couldn't eat, see a fashion show, and get back to work on time. Rich's answered with a box lunch show for businesswomen every Wednesday.

So much entertaining might be expected on occasion to put a strain on an organization not really set up as hotels are, for sudden avalanches of hungry people. And there have been times when the public relations office reeled a little from the impact of unexpected numbers of non-RSVPing guests. This happened a few years ago when six hundred Jaycettes, attending a national convention in Atlanta, accepted an invitation to breakfast—and 1758 showed up.

The test of hospitality is probably if they were welcomed and fed. They were. Not only the tea room to which they were bid but every restaurant facility in the store was thrown open and food was found.

It was touch-and-go for a while, though. The tea room hostess wonders what ever happened to the shoes of one pregnant Jaycette who eased her feet out of them and never found them again.

THE PERSONAL TOUCH

When President Franklin D. Roosevelt vacationed at his Little White House down at Warm Springs, Georgia, Rich's bakeshop often baked his birthday cakes. Once on a rush order, Gordon Humphries, assistant personnel director, now semiretired, was called upon to get in his car and deliver the cake personally in the midst of a driving rainstorm. He remembers that Mrs. Roosevelt came out to extricate him and the cake from the clutches of the Secret Service and to thank him most warmly for the trouble he had taken.

Now and then food editors cruise by, wanting recipes. A few years ago Clementine Paddleford, the syndicated food columnist, devoted some space to the famous pecan pies which Callie Williams has been making for Rich's for more than forty years.

Day in and day out, however, things move along at a pretty even, uneventful pace among the cupcakes. People do recall the occasion when a Negro busboy's trek across the roof from the bakeshop to the tea room with a tray of pastries happened to coincide with the display department's installation of "David" on the roof. Some wag had modestly draped the larger-than-life replica of Michelangelo's famed statue with a loincloth. Just as the watching busboy drew up even with the statue the loincloth dropped to the deck—and so did three dozen cherry tarts!

Anything a customer asks looms important to Rich's—and nowhere more so than in the Penelope Penn personal shopping service and the office of bridal consultant.

For eight years, during the time he was Georgia's Lieutenant Governor and then Governor, Ernest S. Vandiver and his wife, Betty, had a pleasant custom of entertaining the capitol press each year at a quail supper. One February day reporters covering the General Assembly realized they were going to the Governor's Mansion that night for their final such party. The next year the young Vandivers would be out of office. The occasion called for a gift from the press. A collection was hastily started and one of their number—a female reporter, who had wistfully hoped to use her lunch hour to get her hair done—was dispatched to Rich's to select something.

There wasn't enough money, there wasn't enough time, and there had certainly not been enough thought on the matter. Penelope Penn was the only answer.

Mrs. David Butts, the poised head of the department, had, as an Army officer's wife, lived all over the world and faced graver crises. She received the problem calmly. It was a time when Kennedy rockers were in vogue, and she recalled that the governor of North Carolina had just given Governor and Mrs. Vandiver a big rocker for the front porch of their home in Lavonia, Georgia. How about another rocker to go with it?

The representative of the press thought it was an inspired idea.

The only trouble was that although Rich's had many rockers of many styles, it did not have one in stock that would match the gift from the Governor of North Carolina.

"Don't worry," said Mrs. Butts. "We'll find one. You go on and get your hair done. The maid will get you a sandwich to eat while you're under the dryer. Check with me when you get back to the capitol."

Three hours later Mrs. Butts had called Rex, Georgia, where a small chair factory makes such rockers, learned that a load had just been delivered to King Hardware Company's store at Lakewood in southwest Atlanta, and dispatched a Rich's truck to buy one and bring it back. She had persuaded the store's engraver to do a rush job on a small brass plate, which would bear the names of the Governor and his lady, identify the donors and the occasion. And the rocker even then rested in the state patrol station in the rear of the Mansion with instructions to the trooper on duty to let no member of the household see it until the time of the presentation.

The delighted, freshly coiffed reporter had but one problem remaining. "The money—I haven't even finished taking up the collection!"

No matter, said this Penelope Penn easily. Pay when it's convenient.

Such service seems noteworthy and astonishing to even a seasoned Rich's customer accustomed to service but it is fairly routine for the Penelope Penn department, which was established back in the 1930's at the suggestion of Dick Rich, then publicity director. From a small beginning with a couple of people Penelope Penn attained international renown in the twenty-year regime of Lutie (Mrs. B. B.) Cheek and continues to flourish under the direction of Mrs. Butts with a staff which at some seasons numbers thirty shoppers.

So well known were the exploits of Rich's personal shopping service during the World War II years that the Post Office Department had no difficulty delivering a letter from a battle-field addressed merely, "Dear Lutie, Atlanta, Ga."

The store took note of the correspondence in an ad, quoting the letter from the soldier: "Dear Lutie, You say you've never met Jean. Well, she's going to call you next time she's in Atlanta . . . says she must meet anyone who can select the kind of gifts you've been sending her for me."

The store added: "And that's how our Mrs. Cheek, personal shopper, struck up a friendship with the wife of one of our men overseas. Happens most every day and we love it! Moral: When we say 'Personal Shopping' we mean Personal."

There was a lot of shopping to do for military personnel during that conflict and those since. But the assignment that still brings quick tears to the eyes of Mrs. Cheek, now retired, was the one from the mother of a boy graduating from West Point. She was a shy, small-town woman and she wanted to look "right" for her son's graduation and the attendant festivities. She put herself in the hands of Mrs. Cheek and staff and they all rejoiced when the mother reported that her son had said the best possible thing: "Oh, Mom, you look just beautiful!"

"That was the last she saw of him," Mrs. Cheek says sadly. "He was sent overseas right away and was killed."

Somehow it comforted Mrs. Cheek and her girls to know that they had helped the soldier's mother have only happy memories of her last hours with him.

Most Penelope Penn shopping is gala and a great deal of it is sentimental—shower and baby-having gifts, bridge prizes, anniversary and birthday presents and, of course, Christmas gifts. The other day there was a woman who wanted to duplicate, under glass, the top of her wedding cake, which had been merrily eaten nineteen years ago. The lady said she and her husband had carefully preserved the original cake topper but time was taking its toll of it and she envisioned a fresh reproduction enveloped in a glass dome as a gift for her husband on their twentieth anniversary.

The bakeshop took on the assignment from Penelope Penn and did very well until the baker got to the ribbon, which held a nosegay of sugar lilies of the valley in place on the original cake. They literally don't make ribbon like that any more, he found after a check. A stickler for authenticity, he took the old ribbon and personally washed and pressed it and restored it to the cake top.

The customer was so pleased she sent the baker some flowers, real ones.

A marchesa wrote in from Paris for Penelope Penn to find

and dispatch a particular kind of dogwood charm bracelet said to be indigenous to Atlanta. An Alabama schoolteacher ordered "one metal Easter egg, candy filled, decorated—bunnies preferred—to cost 19 cents." The order received the prompt attention of Penelope Penn. Americans stationed overseas in all manner of places—Turkey, Greece, Cambodia, anywhere—ask Penelope Penn to shop for them for routine wardrobe and household needs and sometimes to fill vast Christmas lists. Thousands of forgetful husbands have important anniversaries and birthdays registered with Penelope Penn, dismissing the occasion from their minds until they receive a call from the shopping service, a kiss from a grateful wife and, perhaps a few days later, Rich's bill for the gifts.

The department is famed for speed, and once on a two-hour layover in Atlanta between trains on their way from New York to South America, a family of four bought a year's supply of clothes with the help of two experts from Penelope Penn. The father worked for an oil company, recalls Mrs. Butts, and the family had just come home from Europe on furlough, landed in New York, and discovered they had to leave immediately for South America. They saw the Atlanta stopover was on the train schedule, they had heard of Rich's —and the rest was easy. They were whisked through the store, looking, choosing, trying on, and were back at the station boarding their train in two hours. Penelope Penn collected the merchandise, saw to alterations, where necessary, and dispatched the whole wardrobe to the new post in South America the next day.

Recently a Canadian rock hound wrote Penelope Penn and asked for some samples of common rocks to be found on Georgia soil. Mrs. Janie Davis, of the shopping staff, went out in her backyard, picked up a selection, dusted them off, and mailed them—along with a pamphlet setting forth the other charms of Georgia. No charge, of course.

In time of death Georgians frequently ask Penelope Penn

to pick out and send the proper clothes for both the deceased and the bereaved. Friends of the family even call on Rich's to supply what in former years would have been a homemade salad or a covered dish.

"We make up a nice basket that's really caught on," says Mrs. Butts. "Things from the bakeshop and maybe some fruits and canned dainties. It looks pretty, keeps well, and saves a lot of bother."

In addition to the personal shopping service, Penelope Penn directs the activities of the Bride's Bureau, where girls go to register their choice in silver, china, and the like. There is also a vast telephone and mail order division, where the customer knows what she wants and doesn't need the personal attention of a shopper. This functions on the eighth floor near the telephone office, and in season employs a hundred or more people. There are eight Georgia cities from which customers may call free of charge to place their orders at Rich's, but it's a little-known fact that the store seldom turns down a collect call from *anywhere*. This policy might be subject to abuse but, oddly enough, it hasn't been abused.

Help in selecting wedding finery, trousseau, and in getting through that final dramatic moment at the church is a service that comes through still another department—the bridal consultant attached to the bridal salon. Mrs. Cheek, the longtime Penelope Penn, now retired, really started as a bridal consultant and still functions in that capacity occasionally when friends or old customers call on her.

Forced to go to work by her husband's illness and financial reverses in the 1930's, she made inventory of what possible moneymaking skills she had. The only thing she could think of was that as an active member of the Episcopal Church, she had helped stage-manage a few sumptuous, widely admired weddings. She decided to invest some of the family's dwindling capital in a course for bridal consultants in New York. On her return she had just sold her services to Chamberlin,

Johnson & DuBose Company when the store went out of business. Mrs. Cheek was one of the hundred employees who went directly to work at Rich's.

For many years before she became Penelope Penn she served as bridal consultant. She and her successor in this field, Mary Leslie (Mrs. Asa G.) Patterson, have traveled hundreds of miles—to neighboring states and to what they call "Route 2" rural Georgia communities, helping with weddings. Most of these have been the kind that move with the delicate and precise grace of a sonata and are suitably storybook beautiful.

But both consultants admit to awakening in the night and shuddering at the memory of some. There have been times when the bridegroom didn't show. There have been more times, surprisingly, when the bride didn't show.

Mrs. Patterson consulted with one young woman who failed to show up for *two* weddings.

"The third time her engagement was announced I saw her coming and tried to duck it," says Mrs. Patterson. "But she really was a darling and she convinced me that it was my duty to see her through. The third time was the charm—she made it."

Mrs. Patterson started at Rich's as a Junior Leaguer engaged in some fund-raising project and stayed to take a job supervising the College Board. She didn't want the job of bridal consultant when Mr. Rich spoke to her of taking it and would have turned it down except for the advice of Mrs. Cheek, who said, "Now, Mary Leslie, top executives don't like for you to tell them 'No.'"

This was a fact of business life which hadn't occurred to Mrs. Patterson. Once she faced it, she accepted it as probably reasonable and went off to school in Canada to take a course in the practical fundamentals of wedding technique.

There's hardly anything needed for a wedding—except possibly the bridegroom—which Rich's won't supply, from the bride's gown and trousseau to invitations, to candles and mints, the cake, and even the flowers, if the bride wants to put them on her Rich's bill.

Mrs. Patterson's staff varies with the season but when nuptials are numerous, as in June, she can press into service thirty-five consultants, including specialists in Jewish and Roman Catholic weddings.

She herself goes forth to the church many times a week and frequently two or three times on the weekend to see some young woman off down the aisle to the altar. She goes armed with a kit containing a slug of brandy for the nervous groom or the father of the bride, depending on who needs it worse, needles, pins, smelling salts, tranquilizers, such spares as stockings for the girls and ties for the men, blue garters, and her own handsome Brussels lace handkerchief—in case the bride forgot the traditional "something borrowed and something blue."

She learned about some of these emergency aids the hard way. Once there was a bridegroom who fainted on the way up the aisle, after the ceremony.

"I saw him leaning on the girl," Mrs. Patterson recalls, "and I thought, 'Goodness, can't he wait till he gets out of the church for that kind of thing?' Then he toppled over in a dead faint!"

Ushers revived him and got him to the reception, where he insisted on taking his place in the receiving line and he promptly went down again, taking a couple of potted palms with him.

Mrs. Patterson thinks of that young man from time to time but she doesn't worry about him any more. He is the father of five children.

Mrs. Cheek also remembers a few harrowing experiences— the time, for instance, when it was the mother of the groom, not the palms, that was potted. This lady, down from New York for her son's wedding in a small, dry, rural Georgia community, decided to get champagne for the reception. She had to go across the county line to get it and when the hour for the wedding came she was not back. The church filled up, the music was played—and replayed. Finally, it was decided to go on with the wedding without her. The minister was in mid "Do you take . . . ?" when the missing mother came rolling up, merry and drunk, her jacket missing, her hair touseled, her hat askew.

Mrs. Cheek, failing to persuade the lady to wait in the vestibule, finally pinned up her hair, straightened her hat, and sent her lurching to her seat.

Then there was the plump matron of honor who popped her zipper from its moorings just when she had one foot in the center aisle. (Mrs. Cheek whipped out needle and thread and hastily secured it.) There was the white-tie wedding to which the best man came wearing a black tie—"as conspicuous as if he had a parrot on his shoulder!" (Mrs. Cheek whisked out a piece of bias tape and improvised.)

Resourcefulness is the stock-in-trade of these gentle experts. If they are miles from Rich's and the need is urgent they can usually think of something. Mrs. Patterson, for instance, has built up a nice relationship with undertakers.

"If the ushers forget their white gloves," she says, "undertakers are so nice about lending us some from their pall-bearer stock!"

12

GEESE GIRLS, GONDOLAS,
AND FASHION

Dudley Pope hunched over some blueprints spread out on his desk on the fourth floor of the Store for Homes last May and said thoughtfully, "I don't know where we'll get her but we really need a buxom wench."

Nobody who worked there appeared startled but a visitor gulped and said, "Wha-at?"

"Here," said Mr. Pope, pointing to the blueprint, "where it says 'geese.' We need a goose girl to swish the geese through the square every hour on the hour."

A secretary made a note and presumably went off to call Central Casting or, at the very least, Personnel and order up a buxom wench. Mr. Pope continued to pore over the blueprints, which, on closer examination, revealed an Elizabethan village, circa 1580, which he was planning to reconstruct on Rich's rooftop before the first leaves turned in October. Sure enough, in one corner of the diagram there was an area marked "geese." Not too far away was a sweetshop and a flower shop and in a moment Mr. Pope began to speak of ancient oak-timbered houses and leaded paned windows and it would have been a poor listener indeed who didn't start smelling hot cross buns and mignonette from the cottage gardens. For Rich's Design & Display director, Dudley Pope, and his staff are past masters at the art of creating atmosphere.

It is, in fact, their specialty—the feat of turning the mere buying and selling of merchandise into a fiesta, a carnival, a circus, a Mardi Gras. As Alvin Ferst, the engineer in charge of planning, aims to make the store efficient and workable, Dudley Pope and what he calls "my pack" bend every effort to make it a sensory delight—brightening the eye, refreshing the nostrils, and filling the ears with sounds now soothing, now exciting.

The creation of an Elizabethan village on the rooftop was just the froth on a big storewide promotion of British products last October. Every department featured "Made in England" goods and to set it off, Design & Display generated atmosphere that was both old and new—as old as Elizabeth I and Samuel Johnson, as young as Prince Charles and the Beatles.

Elegant English antiques were used throughout the store just to create a mood, and twenty thousand fresh roses were flown over from England to put the crowning touch on the store's decor.

The fall before that, Rich's went Italian so thoroughly and so persuasively that they're still getting mail about it. Michelangelo's famed statue "David" was reconstructed in Florence, along with several other famous statues, and brought to Rich's. "David" stood on a pedestal on the roof, silhouetted against the city's skyline and set off a citywide interest in art, attracting schoolchild tours and thousands of other interested visitors. Some people who thought they might never get any closer to Italy and the original David, made several trips, stopping by the street-floor Italian grocery and coffee shop on the way home to have a cup of espresso, courtesy of the store, and maybe to buy a long crusty loaf of Italian bread and a jar of hot peppers.

So well and truly was the reproduction executed that Georgia State College asked for and was given "David" to ornament their future downtown campus.

A tour of Design & Display's warehouse on Marietta Street and the big cluttered workrooms and loft over the Store for

Homes is very like a tour of a major Hollywood movie studio's prop department. A Rich's fan of any standing can identify in bins and racks and on shelves, props from the big productions of the past, just as a real movie fan can pick out bathtubs used in DeMille epics going back to the 1930's.

There's amusing junk and there are splendid irreplaceable finds from all over the world. You might bump your shins on a plywood lion painted orange (he wore a ruff of real orchids during the "Spring Is Here" promotion), or bump your head on a Venetian chandelier, one of a dozen especially made for Rich's Italian show. You will see an Edison talking machine with sausage-shaped records, picked up in an antique shop in London for some inexplicable future use, and a hollowed-out log pig trough, garnered in the North Georgia mountains to be filled with flowers and used in a home show. There's a rose-painted porcelain lavatory brought from France for use in a bath and bed show, and next to it a tin bathtub that held ferns in the same show.

One of the more spectacular, if cumbersome, props was a genuine gondola bought from a canal in Venice and used several times in various productions. R. B. Eason, who had the problem getting it to Atlanta after it was lifted from the hold of a ship in New York, still refers to it as "that damned gondola." It is over forty feet long and the limit for things hauling across country was thirty-six feet.

"We considered floating it down the inland waterway," Mr. Eason said, "but then we would have had to get it over-land to Atlanta."

The resourceful Mr. Eason, who in forty years knew every conveyance that moved in America in any direction, remembered that the Long Island Rail Road had some old-time freight cars that loaded from the end, instead of from the side.

"They had abandoned them but still had some that weren't junked so we borrowed one," he recalled. "Stuck that thing in the end of it and here it came. Got into Inman Yards in

Atlanta at 4 A.M. and we met it with a flatbed trailer and brought it to the store before anybody was up."

Gondolas are rare in Georgia but such problems are almost daily with Design & Display. If they are not working on some big, extraordinary production, such as flying bushels of lilacs from Belgium to complement the lavender-blue-mauve decor of their own January 1967 centennial celebration, they are engrossed in regular seasonal shows. Home shows in which forty or fifty rooms are decorated are twice-a-year events. There's always a gala spring show with musical combos on every floor, fashion shows, and thousands of fresh flowers everywhere.

Flowers, fashion, music, *and* food are an unbeatable attraction, Rich's has found, and between Dudley Pope and Sol Kent, the fashion director, these productions have become so beautiful and amusing Rich's could sell tickets, if merchandise weren't its business.

Mannequins no longer simply walk down a runway, smiling glassily and turning and pirouetting. They dance. They sing. They do pantomime. It is, Dudley Pope points out, tongue in cheek, provocative, "almost Hellzapoppin."

Every department in the store takes a hand, once a promotion is settled on, and the merchandise is bought with the theme in mind. From the menus in the tea room, to the food, to the wrapping paper and shopping bags, the motif is carried out. Once Mr. Pope had a tile made in Palermo to set the theme of a show and it worked out so well on wrapping paper, shopping bags, and programs that they repeated it on place mats, tablecloths, and napkins sold in the linen department. To his gratification, a Rich's buyer discovered that other stores had been to the manufacturing source and ordered quantities of goods bearing the Rich's design.

Design & Display is a big department with its own carpenters, painters, and electricians, architects, and draftsmen, as well as artists and interior decorators. It works months and even a year ahead on most major productions, including Christmas.

Before the starched white lace of Atlanta's dogwoods beruffle the city in spring, Phil Johnson, design supervisor, has Christmas on his drawing board. The plans will be drawn down to the last ornament on the three hundred-odd trees used throughout the store, the swags of greenery, and the fruit. One Saturday night in November the minute the store closes sixty or seventy people will spin into action and by store opening time on Monday morning every floor will be beautifully, breathtakingly Christmasy.

There is one Rich's production to which tickets are sold—and that's the annual show called "Fashionata." Sol Kent, a slim, bespectacled young man, who became one of the first male fashion directors in the history of retailing, is responsible for writing, directing, and staging this production, which plays to standing-room-only audiences each year. Tickets to it are as avidly sought throughout the Southeast as tickets to the opera because it always brings to town a preview of what the name designers in Paris, London, Rome, and New York have in mind for the upcoming season. They are handsomely presented with a lighthearted, irreverent commentary by Mr. Kent himself.

A great many Atlanta women would like to have Sol Kent guide them through the precarious shoals and pitfalls of clothes-buying, and he cheerfully leaves his office and cases the racks in the Specialty Shop for a few—the ones, he specifies, whose wardrobes he already knows. His value, he maintains, is "a fantastic memory for trivia" and an ability to fit the new with the old. (One of his favorite axioms is: "There's nothing so unchic as a woman who looks too *new*.")

Occasionally, he can be prevailed upon to lend a hand to a hard-pressed newcomer. When Martin Luther King, the Negro civil rights leader, was going to Sweden to accept the Nobel Peace Prize, a friend asked Sol if he would help Mrs.

King select her clothes for the occasion. Mr. Kent deprecated his assistance to Mrs. King, who is not only a beautiful woman but one of natural chic. But he did make a suggestion or two. On the theory that she was going to a clime where fine furs are so common as to be almost banal, he suggested that she wear a cloth coat and Mrs. King did.

As a fashion arbiter, Sol Kent's background would seem to be even more unlikely than that of his predecessor, the late Miss Annie Mae Gallagher, daughter of a policeman. He grew up in Columbus, Georgia, and majored in English at the University of Chicago, working during summer vacations in a machine shop in Jordan Cotton Mills for ten dollars a week.

For one whole summer he drilled holes in metal pipes. The next summer he looked for something cooler and found a berth in the rug and drapery department of Kirven's Department Store. One assignment was to take inventory of all the drapery pins. Even in so uncongenial a job, Mr. Kent showed a perverse efficiency. He put a pound of pins on a scale and then counted them, thus polishing off the inventory in nothing flat by weighing instead of counting the rest of the pins.

In other summers he worked in receiving, ticketing merchandise, and then in display. By the time he was out of college the store had a place for him in advertising, and he went from there to being a buyer. In 1947 he convinced the store that he should go to Paris to see the couturier collections. What he saw left such a profound impression on him that he wangled enough models by Balenciaga, Dior, Jacques Fath, Lucien LeLong and Patou to stage the store's first topflight fashion show.

"It was a real big fashion show," Mr. Kent observes artlessly.

He made what some merchants would regard as a serious mistake. He was attracted to Claire McCardell designs and bought a great many, which Columbus women resisted valorously.

"I took tremendous markdowns on them," he recalls, "and went back and bought more Claire McCardells."

This time his faith in the designer or perhaps his persistence won through. The dresses were snapped up immediately.

Meanwhile, Sol married a young woman he met in fashion, the former Irene Fried, and they learned Rich's was looking for a fashion director. That was in 1949, following the retirement of Miss Gallagher. Sol applied and has been with Rich's since. It amuses him, as the father of two sons, to go to an AMC meeting of fashion directors and find himself the only male there—"twenty-seven ladies and me"—but he thinks men belong in the business.

They have the necessary objectivity, he believes, to divorce themselves from the clothes—an impossible feat for a woman, who is inclined to look for what might be becoming to her.

Credited by many with creating a renascence in fashion in the South, Sol Kent denies it. Rich's has always been astute about fashion, he says, and attributes it mostly to the taste and concern for quality of the proprietors. Besides, says Mr. Kent, smiling, there are no more regional or provincial colloquialisms in clothes, no more country bumpkins.

"Women of chic in the Southeast basically dress like women of chic anywhere else in the whole wide world," he says.

Even so, chic is not likely to be so all-pervasive that Dudley Pope will ever have to import buxom geese girls when they are needed.

13

THE GREAT TREE

A couple of summers ago when James Rickerson of Rich's
Poster Department had to go to the hospital for several days
a well-meaning and orderly young secretary decided to surprise him by cleaning up his office.

To the alien eye the Poster Department looks cluttered any-
how, and Mr. Rickerson's desk was the kind of mess to bring
out the housewifely instincts of any woman. Why, there
were dog-eared, pencil-smudged scraps of paper there that
must have been there for years!

Now it's not clear if those scraps of paper were swept into
the trash bin or collected and tidily filed in some limbo
known only to neophyte secretaries. All they remember at
Rich's is that when Jimmy Rickerson returned to his desk
they nearly had to call an ambulance and reengage his room
at the hospital.

Mr. Rickerson took a look and said hoarsely, "The Trees.
Where are The Trees?"

Now there are trees and trees but when anybody at Rich's
speaks of a Tree with a capital "T" you can tell. They mean
the big tree—the great big tree—which will tower above the
store during the Christmas season, ceremonially lighted in the
presence of hundreds of thousands of Georgians Thanksgiving night.

It is a project which has Mr. Rickerson's most ardent attention from May to November, and that grubby little collection of papers on his desk had contained an eighteen years' accumulation of his blue-ribbon prospects for The Great Tree.

When asked about it now Jimmy Rickerson shudders slightly and changes the subject. But his co-workers well remember that he donned coveralls and went down to the underground bowels of the store, where they collect and bale for salvage sale all the scrap paper. For two days and two nights he sorted through damp paper towels, limp paper bags, greasy paper napkins and old memos and order blanks—searching, searching.

In the end he had to give up and start over again. But, as Shakespeare pointed out, the uses of adversity can be sweet, and they do say that when 150,000 Georgians lifted their faces to the sky Thanksgiving night that year they saw the lights go on on the prettiest tree of all.

With the passage of the years the exact origin of this Rich's spectacular has entered the realm of legend. Some people say that Joseph Guillozet, an imaginative man who headed the advertising department at the time, got the idea. Many Atlantans will tell you that an obscure little secretary, no longer at the store, suggested it. Jimmy Rickerson himself recalls that Frank Pallotta, onetime head of the Design & Display Department, left the building one night, looked at the bridge spanning Forsyth Street between the main store and the Store for Homes and said, "God, what a place for a Christmas tree!"

Whatever the origin, every Christmas since 1948 people approaching Atlanta from any direction have seen high on the skyline the shimmering lighted presence of a real Christmas tree.

Dick Rich himself is responsible for the fact that there was so ideal a place to put a Christmas tree. He was serving in the Air Force and on a special Foreign Economic Administration mission in Brazil, when he dropped a memo back to the folks at home, outlining an idea he had. He visualized an entire new store building especially designed and equipped to concentrate on home furnishings, and he thought it ought to be across Forsyth Street, connected to the main store by a bridge.

That bridge, which the store likes to call "the Crystal Bridge," houses many things at different seasons—eating places, shoes, furniture, and once during a big Italian promotion, a series of small shops patterned after those on the famed bridge in Florence, Italy. But during the Christmas season its glass walls become stained-glass windows and on Thanksgiving night it is a glorified, four-story choir loft, from which several hundred of the city's best choristers take turns singing the old and well-loved Christmas carols.

Long before this night, however, Jimmy Rickerson has been involved in a search and in a logistical operation that would do credit to the United States Army Engineers.

First, he has to find a tree. He has—or had—a private list of those he has seen in the past and knew would be "right" for some future year. In addition, he has a sizable amount of correspondence from people who either have a tree to sell or from tipsters who have seen a particularly attractive prospect.

An old lady, ninety years old, writes in that she has a tree she will swap to Rich's for goods. "I need so many things worse than I need that old cedar in the pasture. . . . Send your men that hunt trees to see me."

A South Carolina man whose tree they tried to buy a few years ago writes that his wife wouldn't let him sell then but she has changed her mind. "She says though, she wouldn't let anybody but Rich's have our tree at any price. P.S. It's a little sparser than when you saw it, due to blight."

The most common failing among tree owners is overestimating the stature of their cedars and pines. Seldom does Mr. Rickerson hear from an owner who doesn't estimate his tree as seventy feet tall, even if it is a scant thirty.

Even so, Jimmy says, "I keep every one that is at all possible under surveillance."

It's September and still hot when Jimmy starts out on the tree hunt, covering the mountains of north Georgia, North and South Carolina, Tennessee, and sometimes Kentucky. The search takes three or four weeks, running up to two thousand miles, and when a tree is finally spotted its dimensions are as carefully checked as those of any Miss America. The tree—The Great Tree, that is—should be at least sixty feet tall (some have been seventy feet). It should have a spread of thirty-five feet at its base and taper upward symmetrically. White pines have been the choice of most years, but cedars and even spruces are acceptable. Youth is as important to a tree as to a beauty queen. It should be twenty-five to thirty years old, to have attained the right size, and still retain the resilience which will keep its branches from breaking under a load of lights and ornaments.

All this size, beauty, and symmetry, however, would come to nought if the tree should be in a place where the moving crews with their cables and crane and lowboy couldn't operate. So, as with Miss America, there are alternates—two or three potential trees. When the moving contractor has surveyed the territory and made sure he can get the tree out without damage to it or the surrounding terrain, it is marked, an agreement is signed with the owner, and money changes hands—usually around $100, sometimes up to $250, the least expensive thing about the tree.

Actual moving takes place the middle of November. The tree is outfitted with a girdle to keep the cables from damaging its trunk, and it is then tenderly cut and lifted by a twenty-ton crane to the lowboy, which brings it to Atlanta. The movers usually get to the outskirts of the city in the late afternoon and park there until about midnight, when traffic is at a low ebb. Then they bring the tree down Forsyth Street, where another big crane—a ninety-footer with a thirty-foot extension—awaits it.

"If the wind is right and conditions are perfect, it takes about ten minutes to lift the tree in place," Mr. Rickerson said.

Before that crucial lifting operation, the electrical contractor has moved in and crews have been assembling the makings of a scaffold, which will envelop the big tree for the artful task of dressing it, after it has been set in a drum of water and securely anchored against whatever winter wind may blow.

Georgia homemakers digging out ornaments for their home trees sometimes read the statistics on the fixings for Rich's "Great Tree" and take heart. The star, which tops the big tree, is seven feet tall and has to be sent out to be cleaned and refurbished each year. There are about 285 ornaments the size of basketballs, each of them containing a 60-watt bulb; 2500 twinkle lights; and 2000 five-inch gold ornaments, which reflect the lights. The housewife's tangle of electric wire somehow seems easy to cope with when she reads that the crew at Rich's is stringing four miles of electric wire.

"It takes about two nights to make corrections on the ornaments," says Mr. Rickerson. "We have somebody on the street with a walkie-talkie to look at the tree from every angle and somebody on the roof with another walkie-talkie to relay the directions for changes."

The tree is going to be up from the middle of November to three or four days after Christmas, and the effort to keep it fresh and beautiful is prodigious. It drinks up ten gallons of water the first day on the roof and four or five gallons a day after that. Vitamins are added to the water, if it is a warm season, and if it should snow or freeze the electricians have a thermostat which will kick on current to melt the snow and ice.

By this time choirs are rehearsing and Dudley Pope, Jimmy's boss and head of the Design & Display Department, has whipped into shape a schedule roughly as complicated and fast-moving as the unloading of the Ringling Brothers, Barnum & Bailey Circus. For the Wednesday before Thanksgiving there is a dress rehearsal, preceded by dinner in the Magnolia Room for the three hundred-odd participants in the ceremony.

Memos go out in all directions—to James L. Steenberg, in charge of food services, to Building Superintendent William Turner, who will maintain escalator and elevator services and set up a P.A. system with a standing mike in the dining room, to people who will escort the various choirs to their assigned places, even to somebody who will make sure racks will be properly placed to hold the guests' coats.

Arrangements are made with neighborhood businesses to douse their lights for the hour between 7 and 8 P.M. Thanksgiving night. Even the streetlights and the traffic lights are off for the crucial period of thirty-two minutes. Needless to say, the store lights are off and store employees use flashlights to conduct the singers, the electrical crews, the sound men to their places, and about 125 of Mr. Rich's special guests, including the mayor and city officials and the governor, to a vantage point on the Budget Store rooftop to see the proceedings. (The night is usually cold and these dignitaries are warmed by coffee and hot chocolate.)

Down in the street the crowd has been assembling for hours. Forsyth Street is roped off to vehicular traffic, and people pour into it from all directions, city people and their country cousins, rich people and poor people, the young, the old, crippled people in wheelchairs, blind people clutching their white-painted canes, clinging to the arms of seeing relatives. There are babies in their mothers' arms and toddlers riding fathers' shoulders. They jam the street, making it a vast lane of crowded bodies and uplifted faces.

Then Bob Van Camp, organist and longtime WSB radio announcer, who has always emceed the program, begins reading:

"And it came to pass in those days, that there went out a decree from Caesar Augustus . . ."

The old story is retold in Scripture and in music, for even as Mr. Van Camp reads, the singing begins. First, the piping voices of children from the lowest bridge at the second-story level is heard and then the music sweeps upward to the topmost choir on the fifth-floor level. When the story is ended and the last choir has sung, a switch is thrown and the big tree, subject of months of planning, hard work, and expense, suddenly blazes with light.

"Silent night, holy night," sing the choirs. And down in the street the crowd takes up the carol: "All is calm, all is bright . . ."

From the big tree a radiance reflects on the faces of children standing below in the darkness and sometimes it makes prisms of tears on the faces of grownups.

Christmas has officially begun in Atlanta.

Why, ask the merchandise majors, would a big store go to so much trouble when there's nothing for sale?

The answer was a hundred years a-building.